LIFE CENTERED

LCE

EDUCATION

A PRODUCT OF THE COUNCIL
FOR EXCEPTIONAL CHILDREN

Life Centered Education

THE TEACHER'S GUIDE

Donna Wandry

Michael L. Wehmeyer

Susan Glor-Scheib

Life Centered Education Teacher's Guide

ISBN 0–86586–473–X

Copyright © 2013 by the Council for Exceptional Children, 2900 Crystal Drive, Suite 1000, Arlington, VA 22202-3557

Stock No. P6066

Editorial Director: Kathleen McLane
Production: Carol L. Williams
Copy Editor: Tracy Pastian
Proofreader: Anne-Marie Konviser

Printed in the United States of America

10 9   8 7   6   5   4   3   2 1

Table of Contents

Acknowledgements

CEC appreciates the commitment and effort of each individual who participated in the 2012 revision of Life Centered Career Education (LCCE) and the creation of the Life Centered Education (LCE) curriculum and assessment web portal. The process was enormously challenging, as it involved not only a significant content revision, but also conversion to a server-based format. Through persistence, constant collaboration, and deep devotion to the curriculum, the task was accomplished. All participants in the revision are experts in the field of transition and drew on their knowledge of transition and special education when making recommendations.

The following individuals served as members of the revision task force, and their insight and feedback are greatly appreciated.

Donna Wandry, Task Force Chair, West Chester University

Patricia Koppeis Burch, North St. Francois County R-1, Missouri

John Castellani, Johns Hopkins University

Jim Heiden, School District of Cudahy, Wisconsin

Pam Luft, Kent State University

Valerie Mazzotti, East Carolina University

Rick Roessler, University of Arkansas, Emeritus

Audrey Trainor, University of Wisconsin-Madison

Michael Wehmeyer, University of Kansas

Each of the individuals listed below was responsible for revising the lesson plans and activities in two or more competencies, with some contributing in more than one domain!

Beatrice Adera

Catherine Thompson

David Lojkovic

Jaime Duran

Kari Bell

Stacie Dojonovich

Toni Cook

The following individuals' contribution to the extensive revision of the Teacher's Guide is deeply appreciated:

Donna Wandry, West Chester University

Susan Glor-Scheib, Indiana University of Pennsylvania, with her team of collaborators, Mariah Shields, Susan Griffith, and Brianne Buchan Reynolds.

Michael Wehmeyer, University of Kansas

CEC is especially grateful to two individuals who were instrumental in every phase of the development of LCE: **Donna Wandry** chaired the LCCE Revision Task Force and was instrumental in every phase of the development of the LCE portal — task force assignments and followup; decisions on revisions to domains, competencies, subcompetencies, objectives, and lesson plans; rewriting the teacher's guide; writing lesson plans whenever needed; and every other phase of the work that the task force accomplished. **Pat Burch** took on the enormous task of leading the revision and field-testing of the LCE assessment tools with her colleague Jenelle Kassabaum. Pat, one of the original contributing developers of LCCE, also wrote numerous lesson plans and was a mainstay of the task force. She was also a constant source of information, teaching experience and inspiration in every phase of the revision project.

CEC is also deeply grateful to **Rick Roessler**, who coordinated the revision of the employment skill domain. Rick is recently retired as a Professor in the Department of Rehabilitation, Human Resources, and Communication Disorders in the College of Education and Health Professions at the University of Arkansas. He is an expert in the field of vocational rehabilitation and was one of the original contributors to the development of LCCE.

Preface

The Council for Exceptional Children is pleased to offer this revision of *Life Centered Career Education: A Competency Based Approach*, now renamed *Life Centered Education: The Teacher's Guide*. Dr. Brolin's original work was founded on the belief that helping students lead successful, rewarding adult lives requires learning not only employment skills but knowledge and skills in all areas of life. This revision maintains Dr. Brolin's original philosophies, but reflects the practices and themes represented in subsequent ongoing generations of transition practice reforms and societal changes. Within the transition education framework, targeted, individualized, process-based curriculum provides the opportunity for children to learn, in the least restrictive environment possible, the academic, daily living, interpersonal, and employment knowledge and skills necessary for attaining their highest levels of economic, personal, and social fulfillment.

CEC supports the belief that transition education should permeate the entire school program and even extend beyond it. It should be infused throughout the curriculum by knowledgeable teachers who are able to modify the curriculum to integrate transition goals with current subject matter standards and content. It is the position of the Council that individualized, appropriate education must include the opportunity for every student to attain his or her highest level of potential through transition education experiences. Children with exceptionalities require transition experiences that will develop their wide range of abilities, needs, and interests to the fullest extent possible.

In order to assist students with exceptionalities to become productive workers and independent adults, special education professionals need to work in collaboration with parents, other educators, community service personnel, and the business community. The LCE approach serves as a model for making this happen.

The author of the original LCCE program, Donn E. Brolin, who died in 1996, dedicated his professional life to the development of materials in support of the concept. The curriculum is the foundation for life skills and transition education for thousands of young people each year. Drawing upon the experience and expertise of practitioners and the professional colleagues of Dr. Brolin, CEC is proud to continue his legacy through an ever-evolving Life Centered Education line of products and services.

Chapter 1
TRANSITION EDUCATION

Transition from secondary education to adulthood represents a period during which adolescents with disabilities face multiple responsibilities and changing roles that include establishing independence, attending postsecondary education or training, developing social networks, choosing a career, participating in their communities, and managing healthcare and financial affairs (Wehmeyer & Webb, 2012). The Life Centered Education (LCE) Curriculum provides a comprehensive instruction and assessment approach to meeting the transition needs of students and federal requirements related to transition education.

The concept of transition typically implies movement and change. Change, as it applies to students who are preparing to leave high school, is associated with new situations that come with demands and challenges that require an array of knowledge and skill sets to function successfully. The idea of planning for one's future seems straightforward and not too complicated until one engages the many facets of this process. The transition to the world after high school is complicated and needs systematic attention.

VERTICAL AND HORIZONTAL TRANSITIONS

Students will experience many transitions throughout their lives. Some of them are predictable and others are unique to individual circumstances. Clark and Patton (2006) described these transitions as vertical (e.g., life span-related and predictable) or horizontal (unique to individual circumstances).

The life span-related (i.e., vertical) transitions are associated with predictable life events, such as beginning school, leaving school, and growing older. Coordinated planning for these transitions can minimize the anxiety that may arise, and make such transitions smoother, but, in reality, little comprehensive planning occurs in the lives of most individuals.

Horizontal transitions refer to movement from one situation or setting to another. One of the most important and frequently discussed horizontal transitions is the movement from separate settings to more inclusive ones. This is an example of a transition that is not age specific, as opportunities for such movement are available throughout the life span for persons with disabilities (Wehmeyer & Patton, 2012).

TRANSITION DEFINED

Transition from school to postschool settings has been defined in different ways, since its inception in the early 1980s. The Division on Career Development and Transition developed one of the most comprehensive definitions. This definition underscores the realities associated with change. It points out that, as students leave school, they will have to assume a variety of adult roles in the community. It also stresses the proactive aspects of transition education and the importance of actively involving students in this process whenever possible. The definition, written by Halpern (1994), reads as follows:

> Transition refers to a change in status from behaving primarily as a student to assuming emergent adult roles in the community. These roles include employment, participating in postsecondary education, maintaining a home, becoming appropriately involved in the community, and experiencing satisfactory personal and social relationships. The process of enhancing transition involves the participation and coordination of school programs, adult agency services, and natural supports within the community. The foundations for transition should be laid during the elementary and middle school years, guided by the broad concept of career development. Transition planning should begin no later than age 14, and students should be encouraged, to the full extent of their capabilities, to assume a maximum amount of responsibility for such planning. (p. 117)

The Individuals with Disabilities Education Act (IDEA), the federal law requiring all students with disabilities to receive a free, appropriate public education, has, since 1990, also required the educational programs of adolescents with disabilities receiving special education services to include a focus on services and instructional needs to enable the student to "transition" from secondary education to postsecondary education and adult life. The term "transition" refers, generally, to the "life changes, adjustments, and cumulative experiences that occur in the lives of young adults as they move from school environments to independent living and work environments" (Wehman, 2006, p. 4).

The 2004 reauthorization of IDEA required that transition services be considered for all students receiving special education services ages 16 and over, although many state plans place the age at 14, and defined "transition services" as a coordinated set of activities for a child with a disability that:

- Is designed to be within a results-oriented process, that is focused on improving the academic and functional achievement of the child with a disability to facilitate the child's movement from school to postschool activities, including postsecondary education, vocational education, integrated employment (including supported employment); continuing and adult education, adult services, independent living, or community participation;
- Is based on the individual child's needs, taking into account the child's strengths, preferences, and interests; and
- Includes instruction, related services, community experiences, the development of employment and other postschool adult living objectives, and, if appropriate, acquisition of daily living skills and functional vocational evaluation [34 CFR 300.43 (a)] [20 U.S.C. 1401(34)].

HISTORICAL PERSPECTIVES

The history of the transition movement, and the history of the LCE Curriculum, reaches as far back as the 1950s and 1960s, with the establishment of the career education movement, into the transition focus of the 1980s and 1990s brought about by the addition of transition mandates to the 1990 amendments to IDEA, and into the secondary school reform movement.

With regard to the latter (career education movement), Johnson (2012) has documented that beginning in the late 1950s, programs involving financing from special education and vocational rehabilitation programs were emerging, creating Cooperative School Vocational Rehabilitation Programs and resulting in the hiring of vocational adjustment coordinators (VACs) who worked in schools with a career and vocational education focus. The Vocational Rehabilitation (VR) Acts of 1968 and 1973 provided additional funds to promote employment for people with disabilities, and, in particular, Section 504 of the VR Act of 1973 provided impetus for a focus on employment outcomes for adolescents and adults with disabilities (Johnson, 2012).

Bassett and Kochhar-Bryant (2012) noted that the career education movement in the United States gained additional momentum in the 1960s when it became a high priority of the U.S. Office of Education's Bureau of Adult, Vocational, and Technical Education, which maintained, extended, and improved upon existing programs of vocational education. As Donn Brolin (1993) documented in the original version of the *LCCE Teacher's Guide*, in 1971 the U.S. Commissioner of Education, Sidney Marland, Jr., proclaimed career education as a major educational reform (Kokaska & Brolin, 1985).

In 1984, the passage of the Carl D. Perkins Vocational Education Act required states to ensure that covered populations of students, including students with disabilities, have access to vocational education (Bassett & Kochhar-Bryant, 2012; Johnson, 2012). In the mid-1980s, toward the end of what Bassett and Kochhar-Bryant identified as the first generation of the transition movement — efforts that began with the aforementioned career and vocational rehabilitation initiatives and furthered through the work of career and vocational pioneers like Clark (Clark, Carlson, Cook, & D'Alonzo, 1991) and Brolin (1993) — under the leadership of Will (1984) and drawing from theoretical and research efforts by Halpern (1985) and others, the need and framework for a systematic approach to promoting transition outcomes emerged, including the previously emphasized employment outcomes but also as community living, postsecondary education, and recreation and leisure outcomes. The culminating inclusion of the transition mandates in the 1990 reauthorization of IDEA established transition services as critical for all students with disabilities.

The 1990s brought a second generation of the transition movement (Bassett & Kocchar-Bryant, 2012). Standards-based reform efforts in the public schools combined, according to Bassett and Kochhar-Bryant, with five events to contribute to the expansion of the transition initiative. These events included the passage of the Americans with Disabilities Act in 1990, a growing body of research linking transition services and more positive postsecondary outcomes for youth with disabilities, federally funded statewide transition initiatives, further amendments to the Vocational Rehabilitation Act to strengthen collaboration with schools and transition services, and the passage of the School to Work Opportunities Act of 1994.

With the new millennium came a third generation of transition services, now explicitly grounded in secondary school reform. The importance of academic outcomes to success in the transition domain was emphasized (Kochhar-Bryant & Bassett, 2004; Wehmeyer, Field, Doren, Jones & Mason, 2004), and, consistent with trends in education research, the focus turned to evidence-based practices in the field (Test, Mazzotti, Mustian, Fowler, Kortering, & Kohler, 2009). The LCE has been revised to reflect the practices and themes represented in this third generation of transition practices, as described subsequently.

IMPORTANCE OF TRANSITION SERVICES

As noted in the previous section, the transition movement in the education of children with disabilities has a long history, both in policy and practice. Is such an extensive focus on transition warranted and, if so, has there been progress since the 1990s when the second generation transition movement emerged? One of the impetuses to the second generation initiatives were findings from research published in the late and mid-1980s that made it clear that students with disabilities were not achieving the types of transition-related outcomes desired. As the first generation of students with disabilities who received educational programming under what is now referred to as the IDEA began to graduate and leave school in the mid-1980s, a number of follow-up and follow-along studies were funded to track graduates and school leavers and to examine adult outcomes for these young people. Chadsey-Rusch, Rusch and O'Reilly (1991) reviewed these studies, examining the research on employment, residential, and social/interpersonal relationship outcomes for youth with disabilities who made the transition from school to adulthood, and concluded:

> The outcomes experienced by youth with disabilities for employment, residential status, and social and interpersonal relationships are disappointing. Although rates vary from state to state, most youths with disabilities are either not employed or underemployed. Few youths live independently, many are not well integrated into their communities, and some appear to be lonely. Overall, youths with disabilities face a very uncertain future that holds little promise of improving as they age (p. 28).

The National Longitudinal Transition Study of Special Education Students (NLTS), sponsored by the U.S. Department of Education, Office of Special Education Programs and running from 1985 to 1993, provided data regarding the adult outcomes of more than 8,000 youth with disabilities. This longitudinal study used a weighted sample which generalized to youth with disabilities across the nation (Blackorby & Wagner, 1996). The findings reinforced the need to focus more attention on transition-related outcomes and to identify practices that would better enable students with disabilities to become self-sufficient young people.

- The rate of competitive employment for youth with disabilities lagged significantly behind the employment rate of youth in the general population both 2 years after high school (46% to 59%) and 3 to 5 years out of school (57% to 69%).
- Gender, type of disability and ethnic background all impacted the probability that students would be competitively employed.
- Only 9% of competitively employed youth with disabilities 2 years out of school earned greater than $6.00 per hour, and that percentage grew to only 40% by 3 to 5 years.
- Only 14% of youth with disabilities who had been out of school for 2 years reported that they attended some type of post-secondary school compared with 53% of youth in the general population. At 3 to 5 years, 27% of youth reported having been involved in postsecondary education at some time after leaving secondary school, compared with 68% of peers in the general population.
- Thirty-three percent of youth in the general population were living independently less than 2 years after graduation, compared with 13% of youth with disabilities. By 3 to 5 years, 60% of nondisabled youth lived independently, compared with 37% of youth with disabilities.

Findings from the NLTS, along with results from numerous follow-up and follow-along studies, provided, as noted previously, the impetus during the 1990 reauthorization of IDEA to include requirements for documenting and providing transition services.

The federal and state focus on transition services over the past 20 years has, clearly, paid some dividends. A second National Longitudinal Transition Study, this one lasting 10 years, from 2000 to 2010, compared the outcomes of a nationally representative sample of over 10,000 youth with disabilities ages 13 to 16 years old with findings from the first NLTS. Newman, Wagner, Cameto, Knokey, and Shaver (2010) reported from this study that:

- Postsecondary enrollment rates were 19% higher in 2005 (46%) than in 1990 (26%) for youth with disabilities.
- Youth with disabilities were more likely to have been reported to be employed and/or attending postsecondary school at the time of the 2005 interview, as compared with the 1990 interview (86% vs. 65%, a 21 percentage point difference).
- Youth with disabilities were more likely to have a savings account in 2005 (56%) than in 1990 (44%).
- Reported rates of youth with disabilities participating in volunteer or community service activities were higher in 2005 (25%) than in 1990 (13%).

Unfortunately, the changes from 1990 to 2005 were not uniformly positive:

- Youth with disabilities as a whole did not vary significantly between 1990 (62%) and 2005 (56%) in their reported employment status, job duration (15 months and 13 months, respectively), hours employed per week (38 hours and 35 hours), type of job, and average wages ($9.10 and $9.00, after adjusting 1990 wages for inflation).
- In 1990, youth with disabilities were more likely to report receiving paid vacation or sick leave, compared to 2005 (60% vs. 38%).

It is clear that a concentrated focus on promoting the transition of youth from secondary education to postsecondary education and adulthood remains a critical component of the education of all youth with disabilities.

PRACTICES AND PRINCIPLES FOR ADOLESCENT TRANSITION

Wehmeyer and Patton (2012) identified a number of guiding principles essential to the transition process for youth with disabilities. These principles are:

- Transition efforts should start early.
- Planning must be comprehensive.
- The planning process must consider a student's preferences and interests.
- The transition planning process should be considered a capacity-building activity (i.e., consider a student's strengths).
- Student participation throughout the process is essential.
- Family involvement is desired, needed, and crucial.
- The transition planning process must be sensitive to diversity.
- Supports and services are useful, and we all use them.
- Community-based activities provide extremely beneficial experiences.
- Interagency commitment and coordination is essential.
- Timing is crucial if certain linkages are to be made and a seamless transition to life after high school is to be achieved.

- Ranking of transition needs must occur for students who have an extensive set of challenges.

As described subsequently, LCE is based upon a framework that takes into account each of these principles and emphasizes best and evidence-based practices in transition services. The National Secondary and Transition Technical Assistance Center (NSTTAC) has identified 33 evidence-based practices in secondary transition (Test et al., 2009) literature, including the following:

- Involving students in the educational planning process
- Teaching functional life skills
- Teaching banking skills
- Teaching restaurant purchasing skills
- Teaching employment skills using computer-assisted instruction (CAI)
- Teaching grocery shopping skills
- Teaching home maintenance
- Teaching leisure skills
- Teaching personal health skills
- Teaching job-specific employment skills
- Teaching purchasing using the "one more than" strategy
- Teaching life skills using CAI
- Teaching life skills using community-based instruction (CBI)
- Teaching self-care skills
- Teaching safety skills
- Teaching self-determination skills
- Teaching self-management for life skills
- Teaching self-management for employment
- Teaching self-advocacy skills
- Teaching purchasing skills
- Teaching functional reading skills
- Teaching functional math skills
- Teaching social skills
- Teaching purchasing skills
- Teaching completing a job application skills
- Teaching job-related social communication skills
- Teaching cooking and food preparation skills
- Teaching employment skills using community based instruction (CBI)
- Providing CBI
- Extending services beyond secondary school

One of the powers of LCE is that teachers can locate lessons to address almost every one of these evidence-based practices. In addition, the NSTTAC has identified 16 evidence-based predictors of postschool employment, education, and independent living success. These predictors include:

- Career awareness
- Community experiences
- Inclusion in general education
- Interagency collaboration
- Occupational courses

- Paid employment/work experiences
- Parental involvement
- Promoting self-determination and self-advocacy
- Self-care and self-management
- Social skills
- Vocational education
- Work study

Once again, LCE has been revised to provide an explicit focus on several of these critical predictors of success, including the following:

Promoting Self-Determination

LCE has provided teachers instructional support to promote self-determination since the publication of the full curriculum in 1993. In that time, promoting self-determination has become even more important to the lives of transition-age students, and LCE has been substantially revised to address this important predictor and outcome of the transition process. There are a number of reasons such a focus is integral to transition education.

First, self-determination status has been linked to the attainment of more positive academic and transition outcomes, including more positive employment and independent living and recreation and leisure outcomes and more positive quality of life and life satisfaction (Wehmeyer, Fields, & Thoma, 2012).

Second, research across disability populations has established the need for intervention to promote self-determination across disability categories, and research consistently finds that students with disabilities are less self-determined than their nondisabled peers (Wehmeyer & Fields, 2007).

Third, teachers believe that teaching students to become more self-determined is important (Carter, Lane, Pierson, & Stang, 2008; Thoma, Pannozzo, Fritton, & Bartholomew, 2008). In a meta-analysis of single subject and group subject design studies, Algozzine, Browder, Karvonen, Test, and Wood (2001) found evidence for the efficacy of instruction to promote component elements of self-determined behavior, including interventions to promote self-advocacy, goal setting and attainment, self-awareness, problem-solving skills, and decision-making skills. Cobb, Lehmann, Newman-Gonchar, and Alwell (2009) conducted a narrative metasynthesis — a narrative synthesis of multiple meta-analytic studies covering seven existing meta-analyses examining self-determination — and concluded that there is sufficient evidence to support the promotion of self-determination as effective. Also, research documents the positive impact of efforts to promote student involvement in educational and transition planning (Test, et al.; Wehmeyer, Palmer, Lee, Williams-Diehm, & Shogren, 2011) on more positive transition and self-determination related outcomes.

Transition Assessment and Planning

Transition assessment involves a look at the student's strengths as well as those areas that require attention now (i.e., instruction or experience) and those that will arise in the future. This assessment process requires a systematic and comprehensive way to obtain this information.

According to Wehmeyer and Patton (2012), this phase should also involve closely looking at the receiving setting(s) into which the student will be going when high school is completed. In other words, the more the student, his or her family, and school-based transition personnel know about the receiving environment (i.e., what is demanded to be successful) and the existing strengths and challenges of the person who must deal with this subsequent setting, the better the chances for creating an effective transition to this new setting.

The results of a comprehensive assessment process should be discussed at an educational planning meeting that is dedicated to the topic of transition and then ultimately written into the educational program for the student. Increasingly, it is understood that the student should be the one who leads the discussion of his or her transition preferences, interests, strengths, and needs, whenever possible.

School, Family, and Agency Coordination

Coordination can and should occur among key parties involved in the transition process. Such coordination requires ongoing cooperation, collaboration, and, at the very least, communication. The movement of a student from school into any number of postschool settings, such as a job or some type of further education, is facilitated by coordination among various school and adult service providers. Interagency collaboration, family involvement, school completion strategies, cultural considerations and the transition to postsecondary education are all critical to the successful transition process.

Community-Based and Life Skills Instruction

Despite the demand for instruction to promote progress in the general education curriculum, there remains the need to provide youth with disabilities instruction on a broad array of skills needed to function in their community, ranging from independent living skills to community inclusion skills and more. In many cases, such instruction is best provided in ecologically valid environments through the use of community-based instruction.

Community-referenced planning and community-based instruction incorporate several basic characteristics. First, community-based instruction relies on community-referenced planning that is ecologically valid. Ryndak and Alper (1996) identified the steps of community-based instruction:

1. Select the instructional domain (e.g., vocation, recreation-leisure, independent living, etc.) based upon community-referenced assessment.
2. Identify current and future environments in this domain in which the student needs to learn skills and knowledge to better enable him or her to succeed.
3. Prioritize the need for instruction in specific subenvironments in each environment.
4. Identify activities within each subenvironment.
5. Task analyze the priority activities into their component skills.

Obviously, community-based instruction is labor-intensive, and many students will be able to learn in a school context and then generalize skills, but some students with autism spectrum disorder, and particularly students with a concomitant cognitive impairment, will benefit from this more intensive instructional approach.

The domains in which life skills and community-based instruction are needed vary, as is always the case, by the student's unique strengths and areas of instructional need. Smith and Targett (2009) identified a number of major critical life skills domains in which students with disabilities might require instruction: Mobility, recreation and leisure skills, health and safety, money management, and socialization.

CONCLUSIONS

LCE is uniquely positioned to provide teachers the support required to address students' transition needs. From a focus on self-determination to differentiated instruction or technology strategies for teaching transition-related content in the general education classroom, to lessons for critical functional skills instruction, LCE provides teachers with the information they need to ensure that their students are successful. The next chapter overviews and discusses the LCE model and framework.

REFERENCES

Algozzine, B., Browder, D., Karvonen, M., Test, D. W., & Wood, W. M. (2001). Effects of interventions to promote self-determination for individuals with disabilities, *Review of Educational Research, 71*, 219-277.

Bassett, D., & Kochhar-Bryant, C. (2012). Adolescent transition education and school reform. In M. L. Wehmeyer & K. W. Web (Eds.), *Handbook of adolescent transition and disability*. New York, NY: Taylor & Francis.

Blackorby, J. & Wagner, M. (1996). Longitudinal postschool outcomes of youth with disabilities: Findings from the National Longitudinal Transition Study. *Exceptional Children, 62*, 399–414.

Brolin, D. E. (1993). Life centered career education: A competency based approach. Reston, VA: The Council for Exceptional Children.

Carter, E. W., Lane, K. L., Pierson, M. R., & Stang, K. K. (2008). Promoting self-determinatoin for transition-age youth: Views of high school general and special educators. *Exceptional Children, 75*(1), 55-70.

Chadsey-Rusch, J., Rusch, F., & O'Reilly, M. F. (1991). Transition from school to integrated communities. *Remedial and Special Education, 12*, 23 – 33.

Clark, G., Carlson, B., Fisher, S., Cook, I., & D'Alonzo, B. (1991). Career development for students with disabilities in elementary schools: A position statement of the Division on Career Development. *Career Development for Exceptional Individuals, 14,* 109–120.

Clark, G. W., & Kolstoe, O. P. (1990). Career development and transition education for adolescents with disabilities. Boston, MA: Allyn and Bacon.

Clark, G. W., & Patton, J. R. (2006). *Transition Planning Inventory-Updated version.* Austin, TX: ProEd.

Cobb, B., Lehmann, J., Newman-Gonchar, R., & Morgen, A. (2009). Self-determination for students with disabilities: A narrative metasynthesis. *Career Development for Exceptional Individuals, 32*(2), 108-114.

Halpern, A. (1985). Transition: A look at the foundations. *Exceptional Children, 5*(6), 479-486.

Halpern, A. S. (1994). The transition of youth with disabilities to adult life: A position statement of the Division on Career Development and Transition. *Career Development for Exceptional Individuals, 17*(2), 115-124.

Johnson, D. R. (2012). Policy in adolescent transition. In M. L. Wehmeyer & K.W. Web (Eds.), *Handbook of adolescent transition and disability*. New York, NY: Taylor & Francis.

Kochhar-Bryant, C., & Bassett, D. (2002). *Aligning transition and standards-based education.* Columbus, OH: Merrill/Prentice Hall.

Kokaska, C. J., & Brolin, D. E. (1985). *Career education for handicapped individuals* (2nd ed.). Columbus, OH: Merrill.

Newman, L., Wagner, M., Cameto, R., Knokey, A. M., and Shaver, D. (2010). *Comparisons across time of the outcomes of youth with disabilities up to 4 years after high school. A report of findings from the National Longitudinal Transition Study (NLTS) and the National Longitudinal Transition Study-2 (NLTS2)* (NCSER 2010-3008). Menlo Park, CA: SRI International.

Ryndak, D., & Alper, S. (1996). *Curriculum content for students with moderate and severe disabilities in inclusive settings.* Bostonm, MA: Allyn and Bacon.

Smith, M.D. & Targett, P. S. (2009). Critical life skills. In P. Wehman, M. D. Smith, & C. Schall (Eds.), *Autism and the transition to adulthood: Success beyond the classroom* (pp. 209-231). Baltimore, MD: Paul H. Brookes.

Test, D. W., Mason, C., Hughes, C., Konrad, M., Neale, M., & Wood, W .M. (2004). Student involvement in individualized education program meetings. *Exceptional Children, 70*(4), 391-412.

Test, D. W., Mazzotti, V. L., Mustian, A. L., Fowler, D. H., Kortering, L, & Kohler, P. (2009). Evidence-based secondary transition predictors for improving postschool outcomes for students with disabilities. *Career Development for Exceptional Individuals, 23*(3), 160-181.

Thoma, C. A., Pannozzo, G. M., Fritton, S. C., Bartholomew, C. C. (2008). A qualitative study of preservice teachers' understanding of self-determination for students with significant disabilities. *Career Development for Exceptional Individuals, 31*(2), 94-105.

Wehman, P. (2006). *Life beyond the classroom: Transition strategies for young people with disabilities* (4th ed.). Baltimore, Paul H. Brookes.

Wehmeyer, M. L., & Field, S. (2007). *Self-determination: Instructional and assessment strategies*. Thousand Oaks, CA: Corwin Press.

Wehmeyer, M. L., Field, S., Doren, B., Jones, B., & Mason, C. (2004). Self-determination and student involvement in standards-based reform. *Exceptional Children, 70*(4), 413-426.

Wehmeyer, M. L., Field, S., & Thoma, C. (2012). Self-determination and adolescent transition education. In M.L. Wehmeyer & K.W. Web (Eds.), *Handbook of adolescent transition and disability*. New York, NY: Taylor & Francis.

Wehmeyer, M. L., Palmer, S. B., Lee, Y., Williams-Diehm, K., & Shogren, K. A. (2011). A randomized-trial evaluation of the effect of *Whose Future is it Anyway?* on self-determination. *Career Development for Exceptional Individuals, 34*(1), 45-56.

Wehmeyer, M. L., & Patton, J. R. (2012). Transition to postsecondary education, employment, and adult living. In D. Zagar, M. L. Wehmeyer & R. Simpson (Eds.), *Educating students with autism spectrum disorders: Research-based principles and practices* (pp. 247-261). New York, NY: Taylor & Francis.

Wehmeyer, M. L. & Webb, K. W. (Eds.)(2012). *Handbook of adolescent transition and disability*. New York, NY: Taylor & Francis.

Will, M. (1984). *OSERS programming for the transition of youth with disabilities: Bridges from school to working life*. Washington, DC: Office of Special Education and Rehabilitation Services, U.S. Office of Education.

Chapter 2
LIFE CENTERED EDUCATION CURRICULUM

The Life Centered Education (LCE) curriculum is based on the position that transition education is more than just a part of the educational program—it is a major focus of the program. The curriculum underscores this point with its emphasis on daily living skills, self-determination and interpersonal skills, and employment skills, all supported by academic skills. This is not to imply that transition education is the only education students should receive, but it should be a significant and pervasive part of what is taught. Transition education focuses on facilitating horizontal and vertical growth and development for all life roles, settings, and events.

This broad life view of transition education is readily apparent in the LCE curriculum, which addresses evolving transition planning and delivery through 20 student competencies in three primary domains: daily living skills, self-determination and interpersonal skills, and employment skills. Instruction to develop academic competencies is seen as supportive to skills in these three categories. While aligned in philosophy with the original Life Centered Career Education curriculum (Brolin, 1973), the LCE curriculum reflects current changing transition education trends. A discussion of each curriculum area and its competencies is presented in the following section.

CURRICULUM AREAS AND COMPETENCIES

Daily Living Skills

The goal of the Individuals with Disabilities Improvement Act (PL 108-446) is that special education services increase the potential for young adults to become independent citizens. They can become home managers; they may have partners, marry, and/or raise families. It is crucial, as it is with all people, that they learn how to manage a home, family, and finances as effectively as possible. The competencies contained in this curriculum area include the following:

1. *Managing Personal Finances.* It is particularly important for individuals to learn how to manage their money. This knowledge includes using and realizing the value of simple financial records, knowing how to obtain and use bank and credit facilities, and planning for wise expenditures. Computational skills in maintaining a checkbook and budget are also necessary.

2. *Selecting and Managing a Household.* Students must learn how to care properly for a home, its furnishings, and its equipment, particularly since such equipment is expensive to purchase and repair. Maintenance and repair of both interior and exterior home components are emphasized in the curriculum.

11

3. *Caring for Personal Needs*. Knowledge of grooming and hygiene methods and physical fitness are examples of information an individual must have to take care of personal bodily needs. Lack of competency in these areas creates problems of acceptance and adjustment.

4. *Demonstrating Relationship Responsibilities*. Students need to understand the components of changing family and friend relationships, providing for the needs of children and adults, and ensuring the safety and health of all family members.

5. *Buying, Preparing, and Consuming Food*. Instruction in planning meals; purchasing, caring for, and storing food; and preparing proper meals is extremely valuable. Learning how to make sound diet choices is an important skill to maintain health.

6. *Buying and Caring for Clothing*. Learning how to purchase appropriate clothing and how to clean, press, and repair clothing should be included in the student's instruction. This increases the durability of clothing, an important budgeting consideration.

7. *Exhibiting Responsible Citizenship*. To become contributing members of the community, students must learn about the laws of the United States, what rights they have, citizen responsibilities, state and local laws, customs, and other pertinent citizenship matters.

8. *Using Recreational Facilities and Engaging in Leisure*. Using opportunities for community activity increase friendship development and self-confidence. Therefore, it is crucial that knowledge of possible leisure activities and resources be made available to all students.

9. *Choosing and Accessing Transportation*. Students need to be able to use intercity and intracity travel resources. They should learn to drive a car, obey the traffic laws, and know the supports that can aid in mobility needs. In this mobile society, it is paramount that an individual be able to get around efficiently for work, leisure, and civic pursuits.

Self-Determination and Interpersonal Skills

Developing independence and self-confidence and maintaining friendships are critical skills for students to learn if they are to adjust satisfactorily in the community. Tantamount to this domain is the ability to engage in effective decision making, self-determination, and communication. The primary competencies that should be learned in this curriculum area are:

10. *Understanding Self-Determination*. Before students can effectively advocate for needed supports, they must learn to understand the importance of personal responsibility and motivation as constructs, as well as the value of generating choices, anticipating consequences, and effectively communicating their needs.

11. *Being Self-Aware*. Students must learn to understand, accept, and respect their uniqueness as individuals. They must gain an understanding of their abilities, values, and aspirations. Self-awareness involves recognizing the perceptions of self as well as others' perceptions of us. This is an important precursor to each of the subsequent competencies needed for effective self-advocacy and successful interpersonal relationships.

12. *Developing Interpersonal Skills*. Students need to be in an environment that gives them positive reinforcement, motivation, and appropriate conditions for learning and behaving in relationship to others. Exploring their roles as individuals in this society, then learning and practicing appropriate interpersonal behavior, enables students to experience social success in home, work, and community settings.

13. *Communicating With Others*. Students must have the necessary communication skills to express themselves and understand others so that they can interact effectively, both

verbally and nonverbally. Expressing one's thoughts assertively and effectively is extremely important in social situations, but it also is an essential skill in exercising self-determination/self-advocacy.

14. *Good Decision Making*. Throughout the developmental years, many children, especially children with disabilities, have decisions made for them. All children must learn what constitutes a good decision, the steps involved, and the many factors entailed in decision making.

15. *Developing Social Awareness*. There are many youth in our schools who fail to understand modes of appropriate social behavior. Understanding the rights and properties of others as well as their behavioral motivations, recognizing authority roles, and demonstrating appropriate public behavior examples of social awareness dealt with in this unit.

16. *Understanding Disability Rights and Responsibilities*. A general understanding of the "laws of the land," as addressed under Daily Living Skills, is essential to good citizenship. However, understanding the specific rights afforded persons with disabilities is key to identifying and advocating for needed services and supports provided under those rights.

Employment Skills

If people are to approach their true potential as wage-earners, they need to become more aware of diverse job possibilities, develop the necessary skills, be provided with varied work experiences, and learn to make logical and viable job choices as they move through the educational system. Thus, early educational efforts must be initiated in the areas of occupational awareness as a precursor to employment choice, job searching, and workplace sustainability through worker "soft skills." The competencies deemed important in this curriculum area are:

17. *Knowing and Exploring Employment Possibilities*. Many youth have an extremely limited perspective of the world of work. They lack both relevant information and experience. Further, they may have difficulty linking their own interests and values to "good fit" employment options. This often results in job choice that is not sustainable. Therefore, information to fuel informed choice must be made available in a concentrated fashion.

18. *Exploring Employment Choices*. Students must become aware of their specific abilities and aptitudes and how these relate to their future life work. Being able to evaluate those aptitudes and match them to occupational options increases the likelihood of employment success.

19. *Seeking, Securing, and Maintaining Employment*. One of the greatest problems students face is lack of knowledge about how to find, apply for, and maintain employment. Students must learn the strategies to secure employment and know about resources available to help them when they need assistance (e.g., state employment service, vocational rehabilitation, social services, print and online ads). Further, they should understand that employment is not a static situation, in that workplace advancement is possible.

20. *Exhibiting Appropriate Employment Skills*. It is important for students to understand that skill at work tasks is not enough to sustain employment. Demonstrating appropriate work behaviors must also be a part of the workplace experience. Too many students possess a false concept of the characteristics of a good worker and do not develop the type of skills needed to enter the job market.

These 20 competencies have been divided further into 94 subcompetencies. These have been further divided into approximately 400 objectives, which are presented in Chapter 3, "Competency Units." The complete competency/subcompetency matrix appears in Figure 2-1.

Domain	Competency Area	1	2	3	4	5	6	7
Daily Living Skills	1. Managing Personal Finances	1. Count money and make correct change	2. Make responsible expenditures	3. Keep financial records	4. Calculate & pay taxes	5. Use credit responsibly	6. Use banking services	
	2. Selecting & Managing a Household	7. Select adequate housing	8. Set up a household	9. Maintain home exterior and interior	10. Use appliances and tools			
	3. Caring for Personal Needs	11. Obtain, interpret and understand health information	12. Demonstrate knowledge of physical fitness, nutrition, and weight	13. Exhibit proper grooming and hygiene	14. Dress appropriately	15. Demonstrate knowledge of common illness, prevention and treatment	16. Practice personal safety	
	4. Demonstrating Relationship Responsibilities	17. Understand relationship roles and changes with friends and others	18. Understand relationship roles and changes with family	19. Demonstrate care of children				
	5. Buying, Preparing, and Consuming Food	20. Plan and eat balanced meals	21. Purchase food	22. Store food	23. Clean food preparation areas	24. Preparing meals and cleaning up after dining	25. Demonstrate appropriate eating habits	
	6. Buying and Caring for Clothing	26. Wash & clean clothing	27. Purchase clothing	28. Iron, mend, and store clothing				
	7. Exhibiting Responsible Citizenship		29. Demonstrate knowledge of civil rights and responsibilities	30. Know nature of local, state, and federal governments	31. Demonstrate knowledge of the law and ability to follow the law	32. Demonstrate knowledge of citizen rights and responsibilities		
	8. Utilizing Recreational Facilities and Engaging in Leisure	33. Demonstrate knowledge of available community resource	34. Choose and plan recreational activities	35. Demonstrate knowledge of the value of recreation	36. Engage in group and individual activities	37. Plan recreation and leisure activities		
	9. Choosing and Accessing Transportation	38. Demonstrate knowledge of traffic rules and safety	39. Demonstrate knowledge and use of various means of transportation	40. Getting around the community	41. Drive a car			
Self-Determination and Interpersonal Skills	10. Understanding Self-Determination	42. Understand personal responsibility	43. Identify and understand motivation	44. Anticipate consequences to choices	45. Communicate needs			
	11. Being Self-Aware	46. Understand personal characteristics and roles	47. Identify Needs: physical, emotional, social, and educational	48. Identify Preferences: physical, emotional, social, and educational	49. Describe other's perception of self	50. Demonstrate awareness of how one's behavior affects others		
	12. Developing Interpersonal Skills	51. Demonstrating listening and responding skills	52. Establish and maintain close relationships	53. Make and maintain friendships	54. Develop and demonstrate appropriate behavior	55. Accept and give praise and criticism		
	13. Communicating With Others	56. Communicate with understanding	57. Know subtleties of communication	58. Assertive and effective communication	59. Recognize and respond to emergency situations			
	14. Good Decision Making	60. Problem Solving	61. Identify and set goals	62. Develop plans and attain goals	63. Self-evaluation and feedback	64. Develop and evaluate alternatives		
	15. Developing Social Awareness	65. Develop respect for the rights and properties of others	66. Recognize authority and follow instructions	67. Demonstrate appropriate behavior in public settings	68. Understand the motivations of others			
	16. Understanding Disability Rights and Responsibilities	69. Identify and understand disability rights and responsibilities	70. Identify and appropriately access needed services and supports					
Employment Skills	17. Knowing and Exploring Employment Possibilities	71. Identify personal values met through work	72. Identify societal values met through work	73. Identify remunerative aspects of work	74. Locate sources of employment and training information	75. Classify jobs into employment categories	76. Investigate local employment and training opportunities	
	18. Exploring Employment Choices	77. Identify major employment interests	78. Identify employment aptitudes	79. Investigate realistic employment choices	80. Identify requirements of desired and avilable employment	81. Identify major employment needs		
	19. Seeking, Securing, and Maintaining Employment	82. Search for a job	83. Apply for a job	84. Interview for a job	85. Solve job-related problems	86. Functions of meeting and exceeding job standards	87. Maintain and advance in employment	
	20. Exhibiting Appropriate Employment Skills	88. Follow directions and observe regulations	89. Recognize importance of attendance and observe regulations	90. Recognize importance of supervision	91. Demonstrate knowledge of work place safety	92. Work with others	93. Meet demands for quality work	94. Work at expected levels of productivity

THE LCE TRANSITIONAL MODEL

The LCE curriculum presents educators with a framework for organizing an effective functional curriculum that will lead to the successful transition of students from school to adult roles.

The LCE Transition Model is based on 12 important propositions that continue to align themselves with Brolin's original construct; they are timeless in their validity. These are as follows:

1. The development of a work personality (i.e., an individual's own unique set of abilities and needs) begins shortly after birth and matures sufficiently only if provided with early and adequate reinforcers in the environment. Thus, it is critical that schools and parents provide early on the experiences and reinforcements that are necessary for appropriate prevocational skills and maturity to develop.

2. One's work outcomes can be defined as more than a job. It may include the important unpaid work that one engages in at home and in various community functions. Thus, one's career is multifaceted, consisting of the productive work activity that one does in the home or as a volunteer for the benefit of the community, as well as any paid employment. For many individuals with disabilities, this concept is particularly important because, while some may not move into traditional employment, their need to work can still be realized.

3. There are sequential stages of transition instruction that must be provided for if the individual is to acquire the necessary skills to meet his or her potential and needs, resulting in increased independence. Awareness of self and others as they relate to accessing home, work, and community settings begins almost immediately in the elementary school and continues into adult life. These are then enhanced by further exploration of skills needed in those environments, and the opportunities to practice them. This principle is the guiding force behind the structure of the lesson plans in this curriculum, taking students through a natural knowledge and skill acquisition process.

4. There are four major domains of instruction that are necessary for successful career development and living skills to be achieved: academic skills; daily living skills; self-determination and interpersonal skills; and employment skills. Academic skills are the fundamental core curricular skills a person needs to access words and data, both key aspects of home, work, and community environments. Daily living skills relate to independent living — for example, being able to manage finances, maintain a home, care for personal needs, and prepare food. Self-determination and interpersonal skills relate not only to knowing oneself and establishing and maintaining satisfactory interpersonal relationships, but also to problem solving, independent functioning, and other qualities necessary for living and working. The final important domain, employment skills, should be given earlier and greater attention by school personnel so that students can develop employment interests, needs, aptitudes, and abilities as a path to future job success.

5. LCE competency instruction can be infused into most subject areas. As indicated earlier, the four domains are inextricably interrelated and often can be taught simultaneously (e.g., important math skills can be taught in relation to an LCE competency). Thus, providing transition programming is not a separate course or course of study, as some still believe. To demonstrate the interrelationship of LCE competencies and core academic standards, LCE lesson plans include direct reference to correlated Common Core Standards adopted by most states.

6. Successful transition requires an active partnership between the school, parents, business and industry, and community agencies that are organized to provide various health, social, psychological, and vocational services for individuals with disabilities. Although this relationship is generally agreed upon as necessary, in practice it has been difficult to achieve. In the LCE model, this relationship is inherent throughout the school years and beyond, not at just the high school level. Education occurs in more places than within the four walls of the school building.

7. Hands-on experiential learning is an important need of learners who have disabilities. Many are more able to respond to motivating, relevant, and familiar learning activities that relate to the real world and its vocational, social, and daily living requirements. Educators must incorporate as many of these experiences into their lesson plans as they can.

8. The principle of inclusion is critical to successful transitional efforts. Persons with disabilities must learn to live and work with all types of people if they are to gain successful work and social outcomes as adults. Administrators and special educators are key to this. Individuals who received services in inclusive general education settings appear to achieve better adult outcomes as reflected in performance in community living and work contexts, interactions with schoolmates and co-workers, independent participation in naturally occurring activities, and quality and size of a natural support network (Ryndak, Ward, Alper, Montgomery, & Storch, 2010).

9. Cooperative learning environments, because they are supported by the evidence-based validity of social interdependence theory (Johnson & Johnson, 2009), promote greater efforts to achieve, more positive relationships, and greater psychological health than do competitive or individual efforts (Johnson, Johnson, & Roseth, 2010). Use of cooperative learning can help students with disabilities acquire a higher self-esteem, interact more, feel accepted by teachers and nondisabled peers, achieve more, and behave more appropriately in the classroom.

10. Age-appropriate assessment is an important and mandated component of successful transitional planning. It may include informal assessments (interviews, questionnaires, direct observation, situational assessments, and curriculum-based assessments) or formal assessments (adaptive behavior scales, specific aptitude tests, self-determination assessments, and interest and work value inventories), with the goal of defining planning and services in the Individualized Education Plan (Sitlington, Neubert, Begun, Lombard, & Leconte, (2007).

11. A Transition Coordinator is necessary to assume responsibility for monitoring and carrying out a successful program that presents instruction in both school and community-based settings; both settings have benefit, but evidence suggests that students who participate in community-based transition programs require fewer postschool supports in the workplace than those who receive only in-school transition services or none at all (Cimera, 2010).

12. Appropriate interagency agreements and cross-agency in-service training are important to secure so that everyone involved agrees upon and understands the transitional program's goals, roles, and responsibilities and the commitment of resources, facilities, and money. Written guidelines should be developed after collaborative discussions and agreements.

The LCE model views transitional programming as needing to begin at the elementary level, with purposeful and organized instruction directed at the development of a work personality and important life skills needed for successful adult functioning. Independent living success depends on the acquisition of a mixture of academic, daily living, self-determination, and interpersonal skills, and employment skills. The majority of individuals with disabilities who lose their jobs do so because of poor self-determination skills and inability to relate to others; they also may have difficulty using their leisure time appropriately, have a lack of knowledge of how to function independently in the community, and the like. A whole-person approach such as LCE can prepare these students for life after school by giving them the opportunity to learn all that is necessary to become productive adults.

IMPLEMENTING THE LCE MODEL

How can a comprehensive program such as LCE become a reality? Implementing transition education means selling change; this is not always easy to do.

If transition education is to be implemented there must be active cooperation and involvement of both school and nonschool personnel (i.e., parents, business and industry workers, and community agency representatives). The total curriculum needs to be sequenced definitively and logically, from the elementary to postsecondary levels. Elementary and secondary personnel must coordinate their efforts to provide sequentially for the learning of each competency.

Transition education requires a shift from the traditional content-based curriculum to one that is more process based, or, perhaps more appealingly, an effective interaction between the two. A process-oriented approach that relates curriculum directly to the outside world and focuses on each student's unique ways of learning and becoming motivated is more appropriate. In process education, primary emphasis is on developing skills; acquiring knowledge and information (content) is secondary. In curriculum development and lesson planning, the key question is: What skills (competencies) are essential to the individual in order to make him or her a more effective person? In process education, the content of the curriculum is selected for its utility in facilitating and exercising those skills. The skills are the goals within the curriculum, the vehicle by which the goal of skill development may be realized. Thus, a competency-based curriculum should be a real course-of-study option, designed to ensure that each student acquires competencies deemed essential to function adequately as a productive worker and citizen.

The proposed competency-based curriculum approach does not necessarily mean the abolishment of courses and structure currently operating in school programs. It does require, however, that instructional content be selected according to its appropriateness for facilitating student acquisition of the competencies. Given the current educational climates that stress closing the achievement gap and achieving adequate yearly progress for all in the academic core curriculum, it is recommended that academic studies be aligned with process-based curriculum. Since the majority of states have adopted the Common Core Standards, it is logical that this curriculum should heed that trend. As the original language crafted by Donn Brolin stated, "the lessons are designed for use in resource or self-contained classrooms, although the activities could be integrated into the mainstream curriculum." Although that language is now somewhat outdated, the principle still applies. School professionals need to be able to see how they can justify embedding of this curricular content into the parameters of the core standards that govern the instruction of the majority of students in our schools.

Therefore, each lesson plan contains a direct reference to common core standards that can be reinforced by the use of the respective lesson. It is important to remember that the role of the curriculum is to guide instruction, not to prescribe the means. Therefore, each school system must decide how it can infuse the teaching of the LCE competencies into its curriculum.

The key to program change is to involve school and community personnel who will plan, implement, and evaluate the new program. Whenever possible, citizens who have disabilities and parents should be involved in the effort. The first step is for a group of interested educators to gain the endorsement of the school district's leadership personnel (e.g., superintendent, principals, and directors of special education, vocational education, guidance, and curriculum and instruction). With this endorsement, the team can then organize an LCE committee consisting of other significant school personnel, parents, employers, disabled persons, and community service agency representatives. This committee should come to an agreement on the basic purpose, goals, and objectives of the program. The next step is to prepare and conduct an in-service training program for selected school personnel, parents, and agencies so that cooperation, responsibilities, and involvement are established. Written guidelines and cooperative agreements with agencies can be formalized afterwards. A more detailed account of the organization and planning for LCE curriculum implementation is contained in the Life Centered Education Training Manual as a component of CEC-provided site training.

THE LIFE CENTERED EDUCATION PROGRAM ROLES

Chapter 3 outlines specific activities to supplement instruction of each set of lessons; these suggestions are linked to adult and peer roles beyond the educator, specifically tied to lesson instruction. However, this section describes in broader strokes the roles educators and other significant adults can play in LCE delivery.

Role of Educators

The LCE approach advocates a change in role for the special education teacher. The teacher may become more of a consultant/advisor to other school personnel, parents, community agencies, and industries by coordinating services and integrating the contributions that school, community, and home can make in meeting students' life transition development needs.

Special education teachers will still be needed to provide specific classroom instruction when it cannot be provided appropriately to certain students in regular classes or community services. However, every attempt should be made, as appropriate to individual students, to infuse transition competency instruction into core academic instruction as a benefit to all students; presenting academic content within an authentic context often increases student motivation and application of content.

Special education teachers will need to advise school and nonschool personnel on how they can best work with each student. The following support will be needed from special education teachers: (a) in-service assistance; (b) methods and materials consultation; (c) modification/development of materials; and (d) sharing of relevant information on the student's basic academic skills, values, and attitudes.

Integration of students with special needs into regular classes is highly recommended, but only when there are assurances that it will be beneficial to these students in competency attainment. A major responsibility of special educators should be to monitor each student's progress and to assume the responsibility of determining where, how, and when each competency is to be acquired. Co-teaching in integrated classes with a regular class teacher is encouraged in providing LCE competency instruction. School professionals are obligated to make adjustments regarding the use of LCE units in light of (a) the needs of their students, (b) varying teaching/ learning styles, (c) factors of the physical and psychological environment, and (d) curriculum standards and instructional policies mandated by the school administration. LCE, in support of the need to adjust to a wide scope of learners, has provided suggestions for accommodations and differentiated instruction to make the lessons accessible to all students.

Role of the Family

Family members are crucial to the success of a transition education program for students with special needs. With guidance and assistance from school personnel, the family can contribute to the learning of every competency. The home is a fertile ground for teaching self-determination and interpersonal skills, daily living, and employment skills. Parents can assist their children by structuring responsibilities, developing vocational awareness, teaching specific skills, and providing a secure psychological environment where self-confidence and independence can be developed adequately. Family members can foster self-determination and problem-solving skills for their emergent adults, and play active systemic roles through participation in class instruction, program evaluation, and peer family support.

Role of Community Personnel

Representatives from such agencies as the state vocational rehabilitation agency, employment service, social service agency, public health agency, rehabilitation centers and workshops, and mental health agencies are examples of major governmental services that should be involved in the transition planning and implementation for students with disabilities. In addition, there are several community service organizations, civic clubs, and other resources in most communities that can be major contributors to the transition education program.

Business and industry representatives are particularly significant in the Employment curriculum area. Field trips and on-the-job tryouts in business and industry inject the realistic components needed in a career education curriculum. Representatives from business and industry should be requested to speak to classes, serve as resource persons, serve on transition advisory committees, sponsor work-shadowing programs, provide appropriate media for classes, and assist in course development. Clergymen, bankers, politicians, firemen, policemen, medical personnel, and other community workers can assist in the Daily Living Skills curriculum area. In recent years many partnerships have evolved between school districts and the business community.

An effective and comprehensive school-community relationship will greatly enhance the implementation of a meaningful career education curriculum for all students. Life Centered Education requires the effective use of community resources so that students may adequately explore and be prepared for the real world.

REFERENCES

Brolin, D. (1973). Career education needs of secondary educable students. *Exceptional Children, 39*, 619-624.

Cimera, R. E. (2010). Can community-based high school transition programs improve the cost-efficiency of supported employment? *Career Development for Exceptional Individuals, 33*(1), 4-12.

Johnson, D. W. & Johnson, R. T. (2009). An educational psychology success story: Social interdependence theory and cooperative learning. *Educational Researcher, 38*(5), 365-379.

Johnson, D. W., Johnson, R. T., & Roseth, C. (2010). Cooperative learning in middle schools: Interrelationship of relationships and achievement. *Middle Grades Research Journal, 5*(1), 1–18

Sitlington, P. L, Neubert, D. A., Begun, W. H., Lombard, R. C., & Lecconte, P. J. (2007). *Assess for success: A practitioner's handbook on transition assessment* (2nd Ed.). Thousand Oaks, CA: Corwin Press.

Chapter 3
COMPETENCY UNITS

EXPLANATION OF THE LESSON PLAN COMPONENTS

The LCE Competency Units enable teachers to infuse transition instruction into regular and special education courses. Rather than constitute all of the activities and information that students should be taught to acquire these skills, the lesson plans provide a basic foundation for the overall effort to teach students essential skills.

The lesson plans provide an organized instructional method for the more than 400 curriculum objectives. The instructional team will determine when, where, and how the units should be taught. Generally, these units are most appropriate for use with students in Grades 7-12 although many of the lesson plans can begin to be taught at the elementary level.

Each of the competency units consists of a series of instructional units, one for each of its respective subcompetencies—a total of 94 in all. The competency unit overview begins with a brief summary of the total number of subcompetency instructional units, objective-linked lesson plans, community and home activities, etc. Each subcompetency instructional unit also provides an overview grid that presents the number of lesson plans, sessions, field trips, instructional resources, home activities, and worksheets that will be required.

The LCE lesson plans address each of the instructional objectives in the subcompetencies presented in the LCE curriculum. Lesson plans for each objective have been written for three levels of the transition education learning process experienced by most students, that is, awareness, exploration, and preparation.

COMPETENCY UNITS

- **Awareness (A) lesson plans** introduce the student to the basic background information, knowledge, and concept of each subcompetency objective.
- **Exploration (E) lesson plans** expose the student to what other persons do in relation to the objective, provide an opportunity for self-analysis, and offer hands-on experiential activities.
- **Preparation (P) lesson plans** present skill-building activities that culminate in performing the subcompetency.

The A-E-P approach is a sequential learning strategy that enables students to acquire the competency level required for mastery of objectives in the LCE program.

Thus, a logical sequence of learning activities is provided to help the student gain competence in each subcompetency area. In addition, use of the A-E-P code assists educators in understanding the organization of the units, as described below.

Coding of Lesson Plans. Each lesson plan contains its own specific code number in the upper right-hand corner. For example, the first lesson plan in this domain is 1.1.1A:1. Reading left to right, this can be interpreted as follows:

1 = Competency number (Managing Personal Finances)
1 = Subcompetency number (Count money and make correct change)
1 = Objective (Identify coins and bills less than or equal to $100.00 in value)
A = Career Awareness stage or level
1 = Lesson Plan 1

In other words, each lesson plan is designed to incrementally address a specific LCE objective. For example, lesson 1.1.1A:1 (Daily Living Skills, Competency 1, Subcompetency 1, presented at the foundational awareness level and the first of a sequence of lessons in that skill) addresses the larger objective of identifying characteristics of coins and bills up to $100.00 in value. The lesson itself, though, is a subset of that larger objective, and focuses on identifying — not using — coins and bills. Since the A-E-P structure is in place, the next lesson, 1.1.1.E.2 (Daily Living Skills, Competency 1, Subcompetency 1, presented at the exploration level and the second of a sequence of lessons in that skill) now asks students to identify value of those bills. And the third lesson in that sequence (1.1.1P:3) asks them to apply those values to purchasing. This attention to awareness, exploration, and preparation is key to the LCE sequence. Further, the lessons list instructional materials needed (including specific reference to those being provided within the curriculum), an introduction (akin to an anticipatory set), a lesson body (aka "Activities") and an evaluation criterion. In addition, it identifies in which roles this skill may be applied.

All worksheets, activity sheets, and fact sheets included in the lesson plans are similarly coded. The coding scheme helps keep materials organized and easy to return to their proper place in the manual.

Instructional Resources. This section of the lesson plan identifies materials and many resources needed to teach the unit, that is, those that are provided and those that the instructor will need to secure. Materials provided in the lesson plans include: student worksheets and fact sheets, instructor activity sheets, transparency masters, and other student handouts. Instructors may choose not to use certain provided materials and may instead administer the questions orally depending on the abilities of their students. Answers to the lesson products are usually not provided. The instructor will need to secure materials such as markers, sheets of blank paper, index cards, telephone directories, dictionaries, appropriate technologies and applications, etc. To provide students with the array of realistic experiences and materials that a functional/transitional curriculum requires, the instructor will need to arrange for guest speakers, field trips, and use of equipment, appliances, and facilities from other departments or agencies. School personnel will need to arrange for and secure the instructional materials and resources indicated in this section. Other materials that the instructor believes could be important to use should be incorporated wherever possible.

Lesson Introduction. Each lesson should be introduced to the students in an interesting manner. The introduction provided is only suggested and can be modified to fit the instructor's style and students' characteristics. For some students, additional orientation and repetition may be necessary.

School Activities/Tasks. Classroom activities to satisfy lesson and LCE objectives are presented in a sequential manner. A variety of individual, dyad, and group activities are provided, which instructors are encouraged to modify to meet the characteristics and needs of their students.

Time estimates for each lesson plan are stated in terms of sessions, with a session representing 40-50+ minutes. Of course, the time needed for each lesson will vary according to the nature and previous experiences of the students. Most lesson plans include one or more student lesson product(s) that will have to be downloaded and reproduced, and sometimes a fact sheet or activity sheet (the latter for the use of the instructor only). Instructors are also encouraged to include additional tasks that would be appropriate for the lesson plan. It is perfectly appropriate to modify the lesson plan and its suggested activities beyond the differentiated instruction tips to meet student needs and characteristics.

Community Activities/Tasks. When field trips and other community-based activities are required, the lesson plan will indicate Community/School Activities. The time estimate will include both the time required for the community and the classroom activity. The instructor will need to spend time prior to the community activity to make arrangements for the class, orient the persons to be involved, copy worksheets, and so forth. Again, the time estimates are offered as approximations, depending on distance, transportation, and other factors. Attempts should be made to arrange as many of the field trips as possible because they add an invaluable reality aspect to the instruction. When certain trips are impossible to organize, we suggest community speakers be secured for class presentations.

Home Activities/Tasks. Parents and family are important educational partners in the LCE Curriculum. Their involvement in and support of what is being taught in the lesson plans is critical to their children's competency attainment. It is recognized that many parents are either not able or not willing to participate in the instructional process. This should not deter attempts to involve those who are able and willing to collaborate. The instructor will need to be considerate of students whose parents/family do not participate while using the results from participating parents for the benefit of the entire class. Encourage students to enlist the help of adult friends, aunts, uncles, grandparents, or other school personnel to participate in practicing competency skills. Every effort must be made to encourage families, relatives, and supportive friends to assist the student in completing lesson products and other assignments. The instructor will need to gauge the level and type of involvement of different families and strive to create reciprocal, productive, student-centered partnerships.

Lesson Plan Evaluation. The instructor should use the evaluation activities and criteria to determine whether or not each student has met the lesson objectives. In many instances a lesson product is used to determine instructional learning. Preparation (P) lesson plans generally require the student to demonstrate skill acquisition. If most students do not meet the evaluation criteria, the lesson plan or a facsimile should be repeated. Evaluations may be oral or written, depending on the capabilities of individual students.

Life/Work Roles. The LCE curriculum is a "whole-person" approach that focuses on both paid and nonpaid career role activities involved in living and working in the community. LCE prepares each student to function in the following four major life/work roles:

- **Family Member**—maintaining one's home and finances, shopping, paying bills, and making good health choices.
- **Employee**—exhibiting responsible work behaviors and being a productive employee/ supervisor/employer.
- **Citizen**—voting, assisting others, participating in volunteer work, and community organizations.
- **Avocational activities**—engaging in productive leisure pursuits, hobbies, and recreational activities such as games and sports.

Lesson Plan Enhancements. Attention has been given to incorporating several new aspects into LCE lesson plans that were not present in the original LCCE format. These are as follows:

(a) differentiated instruction

(b) identification of cross-referencing lessons within other curriculum domains/competencies/subcompetencies/objectives

(c) identification of an interface with the new national Common Core State Standards (CCSS)

(d) infusion of appropriate technology

(e) infusion of diversity concepts.

Alternative Strategies and Tools for Differentiating Instruction. Although the primary context of the LCE curriculum is for use with students with mild to moderate disabilities, there is still an obvious need to incorporate possible modifications or accommodations into the lessons and materials for sensitivity to a variety of learning profiles. Each lesson plan and corresponding provided instructional materials indicate how the differentiation might be accomplished. This may be in the form of modification, in which the actual task represented by the lesson plan is altered, chunked, or reduced to fit students who are not able to complete the task indicated on the respective lesson plan. Please keep in mind, however, that the lessons are inextricably linked to the assessment materials (the Knowledge Battery and Performance Battery), so any modifications are not be so extreme as to violate the validity of those assessment tools.

These modifications and accommodations are not meant to be an exhaustive set, and creative teachers may think of others that are more conducive to their individual classrooms and learners. Again, any modifications must be carefully chosen so as to not undermine the intent of the lesson or its validity when tied to the larger assessments (Knowledge Battery and Performance Battery).

Cross-referencing with other LCE areas. Clearly, no domain or set of skills will exist independent of the others, since the skills are often used across other settings (e.g., a daily living skill would also have ramifications in employment or interpersonal contexts). Therefore, it is beneficial to the curriculum user to be able to easily see where those overlaps occur. This is important, because it not only reinforces skills across settings for students, but also provides a stronger rationale for making this curriculum easier to build into instructional units specific to life skills, or to cluster to embed into the standard curriculum.

Identification of the interface with the national CCSS. Since the majority of states have adopted the CCSS, a new section of each lesson plan represents a direct reference to the CCSS that can be reinforced by the use of the respective lesson.

Infusion of appropriate technology. One of the goals of the curriculum is to reflect changing resources we have as educators and changing resources our students have as learners and as consumers. Therefore, close attention has been given to where the use of technology as a instructional device or as a supporting mechanism for skill demonstration can be embedded. This is not a separate section of the lesson, but is represented as appropriate throughout the lesson to be followed.

Infusion of diversity concepts. Lesson plans and materials have been scrutinized to make them as universal as possible and to not assign gender roles or cultural presumptions. A good example of this is the rewording of the language under Daily Living Skills that originally spoke to responsibilities within marriage; that has been replaced entirely by the use of the term "relationship," since that sets no societal mores into play, but rather recognizes the wide array of partnerships that exist. As with the new area of technology infusion, described in the above section, this is not a separate section of the lesson, but is represented as appropriate throughout the lesson.

SUPPLEMENTAL ACTIVITIES, STRATEGIES, AND ADULT/PEER ROLES

In addition to the lesson plans found within the curriculum itself, the following pages are intended to serve as a guide to supplement competency unit instruction. As explained previously, each of the 400+ objectives that stem from the structure of the 20 competencies and 94 subcompetencies is represented in the curriculum by an A-E-P sequence of lesson plans. In addition, for each of those objectives, the following pages contain activities, strategies, and suggestions for others' participation to supplement the content of the lesson plans. As with the lesson plans, school professionals are obligated to make adjustments to the activities and strategies as appropriate to the learners' needs.

DAILY LIVING SKILLS

Domain: Daily Living Skills
Competency: 1. Managing Personal Finances
Subcompetency: 1. Count Money and Make Correct Change

Objectives	Activities/Strategies	Adult/Peer Roles
1. Identify coins and bills less than or equal to $100.00 in value.	• Students practice with authentic money as much as possible. • Students quiz each other with money flash cards of coins and bills in values up to $100. • Students construct posters of different money values up to $100 using graphic images found in magazines, computer, or online sources.	• Parents and/or peers practice currency identification with student. • Parents and/or peers devise questions or games that allow the student to identify the varieties of currency from memory.
2. Count money in coin and bill denominations with sums less than or equal to $20.00.	• Students practice with authentic money as much as possible. • Students practice selecting different coin and bill denominations valuing $1 to $20 from a container, and then count the money amounts aloud to each other. • Students devise buying/selling games using play money amounts up to $20. • Students play structured money games. Several teacher-made games are available on the following web link: http://www.ehow.com/list_6525765_teacher_made-games-teach-money-skills.html. • Students construct class bulletin board or create a computer-based presentation demonstrating money values up to $20.	• Parents and/or peers give the student different denominations of coins and bills up to $20 and ask the student to count out the combinations. Parents and/or peers allow the student, while shopping, to count out the necessary amounts for purchases equaling $20 or less. • Parents and/or peers allow the student, while shopping and making purchases equaling $20 or less, to receive the change and to count the change.
3. Make correct change from both bills and coins for amounts less than or equal to $50.00.	• Students practice making change with large denomination bills ($10, $20, and $50), using department store items and their prices on flash cards. • Students operate a "store" and "bank" to practice making correct change for amounts equaling $50.00 or less. • Class role-plays situations in which students must make change for purchases of amounts equaling $50.00 or less. • Class identifies all possible situations where knowledge of making change would be important.	• Parents and/or peers allow the student while shopping to select the correct monetary denominations to give to the salesperson for a purchase amount equaling $50 or less, to receive the change, and to count the change and determine if the amount received is correct. • Parents and/or peers role-play "customer" while the student role plays "clerk" using monetary denominations equaling $50.00 or less. • Parents and/or peers allow the student to make change from large denomination bills ($10, $20, and $50) for items listed in department store advertisement brochures or catalogs priced to $50.00.

SUGGESTED LESSON PLAN

LCE Objective 1.1.1 Make correct change from both bills and coins for amounts less than or equal to $50.00.

Lesson Objective: Student will make the correct change for items purchased with $10.00, $20.00, and $50.00 bills.

Instructional Resources: Real or simulated money ($50.00, $20.00, $10.00, $5.00, and $1.00 bills, half dollars, quarters, dimes, nickels, and pennies) and store items with prices marked on them. For variety, choose different stores each time the game is played; grocery store, large pharmacy stores, "big box" stores like Target or Walmart, dollar stores, etc. Be sure to consider immediate locale for authenticity and to follow up with community-based instruction.

Lesson Introduction: Today each of you will role-play being a store clerk for the items that are displayed on this table. One person will be the salesclerk and another person will buy an item that has been marked with the sales tax included. The salesclerk will take the bill handed to him or her and count out loud the correct change to the customer.

School Activity: **Time:** 1 session

Task:

1. Display many differently priced items on a table. Place money in cash register or storage container.

2. Explain directions for role-play to students.

   - Students will take turns role-playing salesclerk..
   - Another student will select one of the items and purchase it with a $10.00 bill, then will buy an item with $20.00 and $50.00.
   - Salesclerk gives the correct change for each item.
   - Students who are observing should compute on a sheet of paper what they think the correct change should be.

Lesson Plan Evaluation:

Activity: Students will role-play customer and clerk in purchasing items.

Criteria: Student will make correct change for three differently priced items when role-playing the salesclerk.

DAILY LIVING SKILLS

Domain: Daily Living Skills
Competency: 1. Managing Personal Finances
Subcompetency: 2. Make Responsible Expenditures

Objectives	Activities/Strategies	Adult/Peer Roles
1. Identify prices on labels and tags of merchandise.	• Students bring in items which have tags and labels that identify their prices. • Students collect tags and labels from purchases and bring them to school for the bulletin board. Class constructs "Items Board" that includes clothing items (record the store where the item was purchased); household items from grocery, "big box," or dollar stores; and grocery items from grocery stores, grocery outlets, etc. Once constructed, students then compare and contrast, and practice making wise expenditures in classroom settings. • Utilizing community-based instruction to various shopping sites, students practice reading labels and unit pricing indicators.	• Parents and/or peers explain how to best utilize information labels and tags. • Parents and/or peers ask questions of students concerning purchasing prices of merchandise when shopping. Representative of Consumer Protection discusses "problems" in reading labels.
2. Choose most economical buy among like items of a similar quality.	• Class discusses the difference between quality and quantity • Students collect magazine, newspaper, and online labels and prices and, with each other, make comparisons in price, quantity, and quality. • Utilizing community-based instruction to various shopping sites, students compare the price, quantity, and quality of different items. • Students practice computation in figuring single-unit purchases when prices are shown in multiples (e.g., 3 cans for $1.59). • Students operate a simulated grocery store to make comparisons of food products using empty food containers. • Utilizing community-based instruction to various shopping sites students go on a field trip to different stores and locate sale items in the stores from their ads.	• Parents and/or peers discuss how they choose the most economical items to be purchased. • Parents and/or peers ask questions of students in making comparisons of the most economical items to be purchased when shopping. • Consumer Protection Representative discusses levels of quality.

Objectives	Activities/Strategies	Adult/Peer Roles
3. Identify purchases as necessities or luxuries in the areas of food, clothing, housing, and transportation.	• Class makes posters or computer-based presentations comparing necessary and luxury items that relate to food, clothing, housing, and transportation. • Class discusses luxuries and necessities in relation to individual lifestyles and economics. • Students collect catalog, newspaper, and online ads that illustrate appeal to buy "luxury" items. • Utilizing community-based instruction to various shopping sites, students compare prices and quality of luxury and necessary items. • Students collect newspaper/magazine advertising for various food, clothing, housing, and transportation necessity and luxury products for bulletin board or computer-based presentation. • Students watch television and online ads and discuss comparative advertising as it relates to predominance of either necessity or luxury items. Students then identify television/radio/online commercials and ads that are misleading. • Students quiz each other with flash cards that picture luxury and necessary items regarding the necessity of having the item. For other suggestions on making smart shopping choices: http://www.themint.org/teens/smart-shopping.html.	• Parents and/or peers discuss which items are necessities and which are luxuries. • Parents and/or peers take the student shopping and ask the student to indicate several items that are luxury and necessary items.

DAILY LIVING SKILLS

Objectives	Activities/Strategies	Adult/Peer Roles
4. Determine amount of money saved by buying sale items.	• Present to class various sale advertisements from newspapers, catalogs, and online sources. Students distinguish between regular and sale prices of advertised items in newspaper ads. • Utilizing community-based instruction to various shopping sites, students plan a trip based on selection of sale items. • Class discusses the fact that, although money is generally saved when buying sale items, often these items are not returnable (e.g., final sale). • Students compute cost of two identical shopping lists, one using regular prices and one using sale prices, to illustrate savings obtained through wise use of "sales." • Students with each other will identify items on sale in the newspaper, the items' regular prices, and the amount of money saved as a result of being on sale.	• Parents review sale advertisements with the student. • Parents plan grocery shopping with the student, incorporating sale items. • Consumer education expert gives presentation.
5. Compare prices of an item in three stores.	• Students develop a list of five different grocery items and compare items' prices from three different grocery store newspaper advertisements. Utilizing community-based instruction to various shopping sites, students visit three different grocery stores, indicate the items' prices from lists developed above, and discuss with each other the store that had the lowest price per item. • Class discusses cost comparison buying practices.	• Parents and/or peers and student discuss selection of the lowest price from three newspaper grocery store advertisements for several identical items. • Parents and/or peers take the student shopping in three different grocery stores and point out any price differences for identical items. Parents and/or peers and student discuss family cost comparison buying practices.

Domain: Daily Living Skills
Competency: 1. Managing Personal Finances
Subcompetency: 3. Keep Basic Financial Records

Objectives	Activities/Strategies	Adult/Peer Roles
1. Construct a monthly personal budget for your present income.	• Students develop a list of budget expenditures (housing expenses, rent, food, bills, loans, cable, internet, phone, etc.). • Students develop a list of income sources. • Class discusses sources of income and expenditures that should be included in a monthly budget. • Students develop a tentative monthly budget that includes all sources of income and expenditures (housing expenses, rent, food, bills, loans, cable, internet, phone, etc.). • Students are given hypothetical financial information and must devise a budget that fits the information. • Students keep receipts of expenses such as medical, utilities, internet provider, and entertainment. • Students keep a record of their income and major expenses for 1 week. • In class activities, students list purchases to fit within a budget using ads, catalogs, and websites as bases for planning.	• Students participate with parents in constructing the family's budget. • Parents require the student to maintain a budget for a given period. • Budget counselor from a local community agency demonstrates budgeting techniques. • Parents and/or peers review with student the previous month's budget and its outcomes.
2. Identify financial information and financial records that should be retained.	• Students construct posters or computer-based presentations with examples of information that should be retained (warranties, sales slips, bills, contracts, leases, wage information, etc.). • Teacher states a situation in which the collection of forms is necessary, and the students develop a list of the necessary forms to provide. • Class discusses appropriate retention and storage procedures for financial information.	• Parents show the student what financial information they retain. • Financial counselor provides information for future planning, tax purposes, receipts of purchase, etc.
3. Record personal major income and expenses for one month.	• Students record all major income and expenditures for a month. • Class discusses advantages of maintaining records of income and expenses. • Students discuss business bookkeeping and how businesses use such information in their planning.	• Parents demonstrate how records help them plan for major purchases.

DAILY LIVING SKILLS

Objectives	Activities/Strategies	Adult/Peer Roles
4. Calculate balances of major debts.	• Students use established debts or mock purchase to calculate balances after regular payments. • Class discusses time payment plans and procedures. • My Budget Planner for Kids and Teens (Windows) — basic personal finance software. For older students, also available are online personal finance software apps.	• Students participate with parents while paying bills to see calculation of balances of major debts. • Credit representative demonstrates how time payments operate.
5. List basic terms used in keeping financial records.	• Class discusses basic financial record-keeping terms. • Students develop a list of the basic financial record-keeping terms from a devised monthly personal budget. • Students explore spreadsheet and database programs for financial record keeping	• Parents discuss basic financial record-keeping concepts with student, including computer-based systems. • Parents review financial record statements with student.

Domain: Daily Living Skills
Competency: 1. Managing Personal Finances
Subcompetency: 4. Calculate and Pay Taxes

Objectives	Activities/Strategies	Adult/Peer Roles
1. Understand the types of taxes normally assessed in the geographic area.	• Class develops a display board showing the different types of taxes associated with their state, using graphic images and actual items. • Class members develop a quiz or computer-based activity with graphic images representing the different types of taxes. • Class members play the quiz game or computer-based activity they developed to determine which type of tax is appropriate for the image.	• Parents identify occasions in which they pay taxes on particular items. • Local Internal Revenue Service representative or County Tax Collector gives class lecture using a 1040 short tax form as a reference.
2. Understand the penalties and deadlines for the payment of taxes.	• Class assembles literature relating to common taxes and their deadlines. • Class discusses the rationale for paying taxes, tax exceptions, late payments, failure to pay taxes, and the penalties established for late payments or failure to pay taxes. • Students explore the IRS website for information on federal taxes	• Parents notify the student when tax notices are received and discuss deadlines and exceptions. • Parents discuss their attitudes about paying taxes with the student and the assumed consequences for not paying taxes or for the misrepresentation of income. • Guest speaker from a local income tax preparation office gives a presentation.

3. Know where to find sources of assistance for the filing of taxes.	• Class discusses the advantages of soliciting assistance in filing income taxes. • Students locate sources of assistance for filing taxes (e.g., online tax preparation services, local tax preparation office, etc.). • Class discusses how to find assistance, such as agencies, lawyers, and accountants and discuss their respective costs.	• Parents identify their sources of tax assistance. • Representatives of tax agencies give demonstration.
4. Know how to complete a 1040 tax form.	• Students establish a mock taxation system: file taxes, audit returns, penalize noncompliance, compute refunds, etc. • Students practice on tax forms (W2, 1040EZ, 1040, 1040A, state and local tax forms). • Class discusses advantages of completing tax forms.	• Students should observe parents filling out family's tax forms. • Parents show the student their previously completed tax forms. • Local Internal Revenue Service representative gives working demonstration of completion of tax forms.

Domain: Daily Living Skills
Competency: 1. Managing Personal Finances
Subcompetency: 5. Use Credit Responsibly

Objectives	Activities/Strategies	Adult/Peer Roles
1. Identify resources for obtaining a loan.	• Class lists possible reasons for applying for loans. • Class discusses difference between necessities and luxuries as they apply to filing for a loan. • Class identifies all sources of loans. • Class discusses the disadvantages of dealing with a high interest loan organization. • Students clip newspaper ads and online advertising sources of loans and then develop a poster or computer-based presentation of these various loan sources. • As a part of community-based instruction, students visit a bank and receive information on loans and loan applications. • Students explore web-based loan services.	• Parents and students locate loan advertisements in the newspaper. • Parents and/or peers accompany students to banks or credit institutions and obtain loan information and applications. • Representatives from lending institutions discuss criteria for obtaining a loan, collateral, interest, etc.

Objectives	Activities/Strategies	Adult/Peer Roles
2. Name advantages and disadvantages of using credit cards.	• Students obtain credit card applications from banks and lending institutions. Additionally, students explore the online credit card application and compare and contrast local vs. online credit card options. • Students identify and discuss terms and conditions listed on credit card applications. • Class discusses the advantages, disadvantages, and responsibilities of using credit cards.	• Parents assist students in identifying key words or terms listed on credit card application forms (e.g., interest charges). • Parents discuss the responsibilities of credit card usage (e.g., payments, consequences of lost or stolen cards). • Representatives from banks discuss procedures for obtaining credit cards and the responsibilities of using them.
3. Complete a loan application.	• Students obtain loan applications from banks and other lending institutions and discuss loan terms with loan officer. • Students identify terms found on loan applications (e.g., rate of interest). • Students create a poster or computer-based presentation listing and defining loan application terms, then review and contrast terms identified on loan applications. • Students role-play the interaction between a loan officer and customer. • Students complete a loan application.	• Parents and student discuss procedures for obtaining a loan. • Parents accompany students to lending institutions to pick up loan applications. • Parents review loan applications with students to identify terms and conditions of loan applications (e.g., interest charges). • Representatives from lending institutions discuss the procedures for obtaining loans.

Domain: Daily Living Skills
Competency: 1. Managing Personal Finances
Subcompetency: 6. Use Banking Services

Objectives	Activities/Strategies	Adult/Peer Roles
1. Open a checking account.	• Students make a poster listing the process of opening a checking account (e.g., know social security number). • Students establish a "bank" and role-play the step-by-step procedures of opening a checking account. • Utilizing community-based instruction, students visit a local bank or credit union and review the procedures of opening a checking account and/or savings account.	• Parents inform student of needed information and procedures for opening a checking account. • Students observe parents paying bills by check and recording them in the checkbook log. • Bank personnel discuss the procedures for opening a checking account and the advantages of paying by check. • Parent assists student in opening a checking account (if financially feasible). • Parents allow student to make supervised transactions with their private banks.

Objectives	Activities/Strategies	Adult/Peer Roles
2. Open a savings account.	• Students create a computer-based presentation of the procedures of opening checking and savings accounts (e.g., know social security number). • Students establish a "bank" and role-play the step-by-step procedures of opening accounts and discussing direct deposit options for their paychecks or other sources of regular income.	• Parents inform student of needed information and procedures for opening a savings account. • Parents help the student practice saving at home by establishing a home "savings account." • Bank personnel discuss the procedures for opening a savings account and the concept of interest. • Parent assists student in opening a bank savings account (if financially feasible). • Parents allow the student to make supervised transactions with their private banks.
3. Write checks, make deposits, and record checking transactions.	• Utilizing community-based instruction, students visit a bank or credit union to discuss procedures to follow when writing checks, making deposits, and recording checking account transactions. • Students create a poster or computer-based presentation detailing the process of writing checks, making deposits, and recording transactions. • Class practices with mock checks, deposit slips, check registers, and monthly bank statements. • Class discusses the importance of accurate checking account record keeping. • Class devises mock checking system and students use checks to purchase classroom items.	• Parents inform the student of the procedures for writing checks, making deposits, and recording transactions. • Parents discuss with the student the family's checking account transactions and recording. • Bank personnel discuss the procedures for writing checks, making deposits, and recording transactions. • Parents assist student in making an actual transaction and in record keeping. • Parents involve the student in balancing the family's checking account.
4. Make deposits and withdrawals, and record savings transactions.	• Class establishes a mock bank and students practice transacting and recording with simulated money.	• Parents review savings records and record transactions with the student. • Parents and students simulate or make actual bank deposits and withdrawals, and record savings transactions.
5. Use local and online banking.	• Class explores advantages and disadvantages of online banking; for more information: http://www.bankrate.com/brm/olbstep2.asp. • Class examines the security process in opening online accounts. • Class explores how to transfer funds between savings, checking, loan, etc., accounts. • Class compares fees associated with live vs. online banking. • Class discusses interest rates and penalties.	• Guest speaker from a local bank or credit union talks to class.

Domain: Daily Living Skills
Competency: 2. Selecting and Managing a Household
Subcompetency: 7. Select Adequate Housing

Objectives	Activities/Strategies	Adult/Peer Roles
1. List personal or family housing requirements, including space, location, and yard.	• In a group activity students identify and list basic requirements of adequate housing (i.e., shelter, living space, cooking and toilet facilities, location, neighborhood, house and yard size, etc.). • Class discusses what needs are important for the student and his or her family and/or roommates (e.g., number of bedrooms). • Class discusses housing needs for hypothetical situations, i.e. having roommates, pets, or needing adaptations to housing facilities (ramps, modified bathroom apparatus, etc.).	• Parents discuss reasons for buying or renting their dwelling. • Parents discuss with students what they might consider in renting or buying a house.
2. Identify different types of housing available in the community.	• Class discusses the different types of habitation (i.e., house, duplex, apartment, trailer). • Students create a bulletin board or computer-based presentation displaying different kinds of habitations. • Students identify representative habitation in the community through newspaper ads, Craigslist, and other media listings. In addition, students explore the HUD website to learn more about quality housing in their locale at the following site: http://portal.hud.gov/hudportal/HUD. • Students, using the housing/rental advertisements section of the newspaper or online sources like Craiglist, select several appropriate personal housing options.	• Parents show the student different types of dwellings. • Local realtor comes to class to discuss housing options within the community.
3. Identify advantages and disadvantages of different types of housing.	• Class discusses advantages and disadvantages of owning and renting (i.e., upkeep, cost, taxes, etc.). • Students develop a personal list of specifications for adequate housing, and make a comparison with advantages and disadvantages of various housing options.	• Parents/peers supervise a student phoning for information about habitation. • Realtor discusses basic housing options offered in the community. • Parents discuss with the student the various types of habitation available in the community. • Realtor presents information concerning the selection of different housing options.

DAILY LIVING SKILLS

Objectives	Activities/Strategies	Adult/Peer Roles
4. Identify procedures for renting a house or apartment.	• Students are given a presentation of procedures for renting a house, signing a lease, paying rent, etc. • Students role-play the rental of an apartment or house. • Utilizing community-based instruction, students visit various types of homes and apartments for rent.	• Parents obtain a copy of a rental agreement and discuss it with the student. • Real estate rental agent discusses procedures for renting and locating appropriate rental units. • Landlords explain their expectations and procedures. • Panel of peers or young adults who are recent graduates visit the class to discuss their choices of renting or buying and factors they considered in making the choice.
5. Identify procedures for buying a house.	• Students are given a presentation on procedures of securing a mortgage, making mortgage payments, making down payments, and paying taxes. • Students role-play the procedures involved in buying a home. • Students visit various homes for sale. • Utilizing community-based instruction, students visit real estate offices or home mortgage offices of local banks or lending agencies.	• Parents discuss with the student their reasons for buying a home. • Parents explain to the student the financial responsibilities involved in owning a home. • Real estate agent explains the procedures involved in purchasing a home. • Panel of peers or young adults presents their experiences in buying a home.

DAILY LIVING SKILLS

Domain: Daily Living Skills
Competency: 2. Selecting and Managing a Household
Subcompetency: 8. Set Up A Household

Objectives	Activities/Strategies	Adult/Peer Roles
1. Describe procedures for connecting utility services.	• Class checks with family members then list on chalkboard the types of utility services they utilize in their homes. • Students research from the telephone directories and websites the names and phone numbers of local companies that provide utility services. • Utilizing website research, students acquire information regarding utility service agreement contracts (e.g., installment deposits, delinquent fees, rates per month), then create a computer-based presentation on various deposits, installment fees, and monthly charges for utilities. • Students role-play connecting/ installation service agreement, telephone conversation, or in-person visit between utility service representatives and themselves. • Students complete sample utility agreement contracts. • Class creates posters or computer-based presentation of the general household items found in various areas and rooms of their homes.	• Parents discuss with student the utilities used in the home. • Parents discuss and show student their records of utility installation agreements.
2. Acquire basic household items.	• Class lists on chalkboard the stores and online sites where one can purchase the basic household items.	• Parents and student identify basic household items in the house. • Parents and student visit stores that sell basic household items.
3. Acquire furniture and major appliances.	• Class creates posters or computer-based presentations of the furniture and major appliances required to set up a home and where they can be rented or purchased.	• Parents and student identify furniture and major appliances in the house. • Parents and student visit stores that sell furniture and major appliances.

Domain: Daily Living Skills
Competency: 2. Selecting and Managing a Household
Subcompetency: 9. Maintain Home Exterior/Interior

Objectives	Activities/Strategies	Adult/Peer Roles
1. Identify basic appliances and tools used in exterior maintenance.	• Students create posters of common tools products associated with inside and outside home maintenance. • Students work in pairs devising a list of basic interior and exterior housekeeping activities involving the tools and products (e.g., wash/dry dishes, wash windows, take out the garbage, use a vacuum cleaner, operate garbage disposal, sweep floor, dust furniture, mow lawn).	• Parents and/or peers identify tools they commonly used for outside home maintenance. • Parents and/or peers ask student to identify these tools. • Member of home maintenance business demonstrates routine materials, tools, and types of jobs.
2. List routine cleaning and maintenance activities.	• If possible, utilizing community-based instruction, visit a "mini-maid" type business or to a hotel/motel to discuss routine housekeeping activities. • Class discusses the procedures involved in housekeeping and the proper sequence in which they should be done. • Class discusses what housekeeping jobs need to be completed daily, weekly, and less frequently.	• Parents assist the student in making a list of housecleaning and maintenance activities in their home. • Parents supervise the student in performing household tasks. • Personnel from housecleaning business discuss the routine activities required in cleaning houses.
3. Outline a weekly housekeeping routine.	• Students work in pairs to discuss and plan a routine which allows a scheduling of regular household tasks (e.g., floors washed and waxed every other Saturday, television dusted every other day, etc.).	• Parents explain to the student their own housekeeping routine and encourage the student to devise his or her own routine. • Maintenance persons (from business, motels, schools, etc.) explain their tools and their routine to the class.
4. Identify the uses of common household cleaning products and equipment.	• Students look through magazines and online resources and identify cleaning accessories. • Students construct a bulletin board which shows different cleaners and their specific uses.	• Parents have the student choose the proper cleaners for various cleaning jobs, and then demonstrate their use. • Member of a home cleaning business provides a demonstration of routine, materials, tools, and types of jobs.

Objectives	Activities/Strategies	Adult/Peer Roles
5. Accessing assistance services and putting in work orders.	• Class discussion about types of household problems that can arise, and maintenance required (e.g., changing furnace filters, washer or dryer not working, water heater leaking, faucets not working, stove burners not working, etc.) and whom to contact regarding repair. If renting a home, the work is often handled by the landlord or rental agent. • Class role-plays situations that involve contact with rental agent or repair person, description of needed repair, and determining and recording date and time repair will be made.	• Parents involve students in their home maintenance chores, e.g., changing filters, fuse or breaker boxes, basic stove cleaning and maintenance, etc.
6. Dispose of household refuse properly.	• Class researches through online resources the recycling procedures for their community. As a function of community-based instruction, class visits recycling centers for information regarding their recycling responsibilities.	• Parents involve students in recycling procedures in their community.
7. Secure home when at home and away from home.	• Class discusses home security and reviews tips on the "how stuff works" website for home security: http://home.howstuffworks.com/ home-improvement/household-safety/security/home-security-tips.htm.	

Domain: Daily Living Skills
Competency: 2. Selecting and Managing a Household
Subcompetency: 10. Use Basic Appliances and Tools

Objectives	Activities/Strategies	Adult/Peer Roles
1. Name common appliances and tools found in the home and tell how each is used.	• Students look through magazines and cut out what they think are essential appliances. Students can also investigate websites for that information: http://www.kitchenappliances.us. • Utilizing community-based instruction, students visit an appliance store and observe demonstrations of appliance and tool usage. • Students construct a mock room or store of appliances.	• Parents introduce and demonstrate to the student all the appliances in the home. • Parents discuss what basic appliances and tools may be lacking in the home.

Objectives	Activities/Strategies	Adult/Peer Roles
2. Demonstrate appropriate use of basic appliances and tools.	• Class lists on a chalkboard the appliances and tools found in the home and in the appliance store. • Students construct a mock room or store of appliances and tools and demonstrate their use to the class. • Students role-play using various appliances and tools not demonstrated in class.	• Parents and/or peers demonstrate how to use various appliances. • Parents let the student use as many different tools as possible within the home. • Maintenance personnel demonstrate various tools appropriate to their jobs and their use in the home.
3. Name safety procedures to follow when using appliances and tools.	• Class lists safety procedures on chalkboard or that are necessary when using appliances and tools. • Students construct a bulletin board which illustrates the dos and don'ts of several tools and appliances. • Class is shown the proper way to handle appliances and tools.	• Parents demonstrate proper maintenance of tools. • Parents discuss the question of safety in relation to using appliances and tools.
4. Perform basic home care tasks.	• Class lists on chalkboard the minor repairs a person should be able to make at home (e.g., lights, locks, painting, leaky and clogged pipes, etc.). • Students take field trip to several repair shops and local hardware stores for repair demonstrations. • Students work in teams on a repair problem. • Students role-play actual performance of maintenance or repair jobs (e.g., grass cutting, painting).	• Parents and/or peers work through a repair job. • Small-appliance repair person demonstrates basic home repairs. • Parents involve students in home maintenance or repair jobs.

Domain: Daily Living Skills
Competency: 3. Caring for Personal Needs
Subcompetency: 11. Obtaining, Interpreting, and Understanding Basic Health Information

Objectives	Activities/Strategies	Adult/Peer Roles
1. Understanding preventive physical and mental health measures, including proper diet, nutrition, exercise, and stress reduction.	• Class downloads the Pennsylvania Department of Health, Transition Health Care Checklist: Transition to Adult Living from the following website: http://www.portal.state. pa.us/portal/server.pt/community/ special_kids_network/14205/ transition_health_care_ checklist/558090.	

DAILY LIVING SKILLS

Objectives	Activities/Strategies	Adult/Peer Roles
2. Using available information to make appropriate health-related decisions.	• Once each class member has completed the inventory, individual plans can be established. The 15-page checklist covers the following areas: self-awareness, personal safety, communication, hearing and vision, medication, self-advocacy, money management, postsecondary considerations, employment considerations, community living, medical management, and activities of daily living.	
3. Establishing and monitoring personal and family health goals.		• Upon completion of the checklist both by the student and the student's family or guardian, personal and family health goals can be completed.

Domain: Daily Living Skills
Competency: 3. Caring for Personal Needs
Subcompetency: 12. Demonstrate Knowledge of Physical Fitness, Nutrition, and Weight

Objectives	Activities/Strategies	Adult/Peer Roles
1. Understand ways nutrition relates to health.	• Students review the latest dietary/nutrition guidelines developed by the Department of Agriculture at this site: http://www.choosemyplate.gov/. • Class discusses the components of a balanced meal and indicates how the meal will make a body healthier (e.g., the beans in the meal contain vitamin B which is good for the nervous system). • Class discusses the relationship of height and weight to nutrition. Students calculate their Body Mass Index (BMI) using the following Center for Disease Control website: http://www.cdc.gov/healthyweight/assessing/bmi/adult_bmi/english_bmi_calculator/bmi_calculator.html. • Class discusses the basic principles of food metabolism. • Each student keeps a personal log of height, weight, and measurements.	• Dietician discusses eating from the four basic food groups and how they relate to good health. • Member of Weight Watchers or Community Health Department representative discusses nutrition and obesity problems.

Objectives	Activities/Strategies	Adult/Peer Roles
2. Be able to design a meal balanced for nutritional and caloric content.	• Teacher displays foods from major food groups, and explains what each food does for the body. • Class constructs a chart or computer-based presentation of a balanced diet for all three meals and healthy snacks, using magazine pictures, drawings, or downloaded graphics and clip art. • Class discusses the body's need for proper nutrition.	• Dietician presents community resource information regarding the basic food groups. Dietician explains procedure for determining appropriate daily caloric intake per food group. • Parents explain to the student how the family's nutritional needs are met.
3. Understand how exercise relates to health.	• Class examines pictures of physically fit and unfit persons and discusses appearances, energy level, longevity, etc. • Class tours a physical fitness club. • Class discusses the emotional rewards of physical fitness. • Class discusses an appropriate regimen of physical exercise. • Class discusses the need for rest in a physical fitness program. • Class lists on chalkboard the ways exercise relates to healthy living.	• Community recreation personnel or coach or nurse discusses personal and family fitness. • Student and parents conduct family physical fitness program.
4. Identify and demonstrate the correct ways of performing common physical exercises.	• Class lists on chalkboard the common physical exercises. • Students are shown the proper execution of push-ups, sit-ups, toe touches, chinning, leg lifts, etc., with an explanation of what body parts are affected by the exercises. • Students examine other forms of aerobic, strengthening, and stretching exercises, and develop practice routines they enjoy and will sustain. • Students construct performance charts that record progress on particular exercises. • Students demonstrate correct ways of performing physical exercises.	• Local athlete demonstrates exercises he or she uses in preparation for his or her own sport.
5. Develop and implement a personal physical fitness routine.		• Parents encourage student to develop a home exercise routine.

DAILY LIVING SKILLS

Domain: Daily Living Skills
Competency: 3. Caring for Personal Needs
Subcompetency: 13. Exhibit Proper Grooming and Hygiene

Objectives	Activities/Strategies	Adult/Peer Roles
1. Demonstrate basic aspects of proper hygiene.	• Class discusses the areas of the body to be cleaned when bathing and showering. • Class lists on chalkboard the daily hygienic activities. The following website has a master checklist for personal grooming: http://www.checklist.com/personal-hygiene-checklist. • Class identifies and discusses the areas of the body that need to be specially groomed, and the grooming products. • Class discusses the necessity of proper hygiene for various parts of the body. • Class discusses the need for oral hygiene. The following website has helpful hints for care of teeth and oral hygiene: http://www.ada.org/2624.aspx • In addition, this website has video instruction on ways to floss and brush teeth properly: http://www.colgate.com/app/CP/US/EN/OC/Information/Articles/Oral-and-Dental-Health-Basics/Oral-Hygiene/Oral-Hygiene-Basics/article/What-is-Good-Oral-Hygiene.cvsp • Students demonstrate the appropriate hygiene techniques.	• Visiting nurse emphasizes the importance in caring for all body parts, including personal body parts. • Parents assist students in mastering hygiene techniques. • Dentist or dental hygienist emphasizes the importance of proper oral hygiene.
2. Identify proper grooming habits.	• Class is given demonstration of grooming with grooming products (e.g., nail clippers and nail file, hairbrush, etc.). • Males are shown the proper use of shaving cream, razor, electric razor, etc. • Females are shown the proper use of shaving cream, razor, electric razor, hair curlers, perfume, make-up, etc. • Class is given demonstration of cleaning ears with cotton-tipped swabs (e.g., Q-tips), removing particles from eyes, etc. • Class is given demonstration of proper use of toothbrush, dental floss, gum massage, and water pick. • Class lists on chalkboard the procedures for shampooing and drying hair.	• Parents and/or peers model appropriate grooming. • Beautician or hair stylist demonstrates appropriate grooming. • Parents allow students to purchase grooming aids (i.e., shampoo, deodorant, cologne, etc.). • Parents observe and record whether student is brushing teeth properly.

Objectives	Activities/Strategies	Adult/Peer Roles
3. Identify proper products for hygiene and where to obtain them.	• Students clip advertisements from magazines regarding products used to maintain proper hygiene. • Class lists on chalkboard the products used to maintain proper hygiene (i.e., toothbrush, shampoo, cotton-tipped swabs, dental floss, etc.). • Class lists on chalkboard the names of stores where hygiene products can be found. • Class constructs bulletin board showing pictures of products related to proper hygiene.	• Parents and student discuss hygiene products found in the home. • Parents and student purchase hygiene products carried in stores.
4. Identify proper products for grooming and where to obtain them.	• Students clip advertisements from magazines regarding products used to maintain proper grooming. • Class lists on chalkboard the products used to maintain proper grooming (i.e., hairbrush, nail clipper, etc.). • Class lists on chalkboard the names of stores where grooming products can be found. • Class constructs bulletin board showing pictures of products related to proper grooming.	• Beautician or cosmetologist and health care professional discuss grooming products and where to obtain them.

Domain: Daily Living Skills
Competency: 3. Caring for Personal Needs
Subcompetency: 14. Dress Appropriately

DAILY LIVING SKILLS

Objectives	Activities/Strategies	Adult/Peer Roles
1. List clothing appropriate for different weather conditions.	• Students clip pictures of clothing articles and paste them on flash cards or create a computer-based presentation using clip art on suggested clothing for seasons and weather conditions. • Class constructs a bulletin board illustrating the major types of seasonal clothing. • Students identify various workers in the community who dress according to weather conditions (i.e., mail carriers, highway repair workers, construction workers, etc.). • Class lists on chalkboard the clothing appropriate for different weather conditions.	• Parents quiz student on appropriate clothing for weather conditions. • Parents take the student on shopping trips, pointing out the variety of seasonal clothing. • Clothes salesperson explains appropriate clothes for different weather conditions.
2. List clothing appropriate for different activities.	• Class lists on chalkboard the variety of occasions that require specific forms of dress. • Class collects pictures from magazines and newspapers depicting people dressed for particular occasions. • Teacher makes lists of clothing and events, and the students match clothing with event. • Students choose appropriate clothes for hypothetical situations. • Class has a fashion show to demonstrate appropriate clothing.	• Salespersons (males and females) from clothing stores address the class on the variety of clothing for particular occasions. • Student observes how parents dress for particular occasions.
3. Given an occasion, choose the appropriate clothing to be worn.	• Students select from magazines, catalogs, and websites the appropriate clothing for a simulated occasion. • Students make a collage of inappropriate clothing for specific occasions. • Class discusses clothing articles that "go together" appropriately.	• Parents discuss appropriate clothing selection. • Parents demonstrate to students their clothing selection for certain occasions.

Domain: Daily Living Skills
Competency: 3. Caring for Personal Needs
Subcompetency: 15. Demonstrate Knowledge of Common Illness, Prevention, and Treatment

Objectives	Activities/Strategies	Adult/Peer Roles
1. Identify major symptoms of common illnesses.	• Students construct a chart depicting symptoms of particular illnesses. • Students discuss how they feel when they have different illnesses. • Students role-play doctor and patient discussing symptoms of common illnesses.	• Nurse or paramedic discusses cleanliness. • Speaker from Public Health Service discusses sanitation and personal cleanliness. • Parents instruct student on the need for cleanliness.
2. Teach how cleanliness is related to health.	• Class discusses the relationship between cleanliness and illness. • Students are shown the techniques of dishwashing as a preventative measure. • Class discusses the necessity of bathing regularly. • Class discusses the need for cleaning a cut or wound.	• Doctor or nurse discusses functions of hospital and office services. • Parent instructs student on how to obtain emergency medical assistance by telephone. • Parents place emergency numbers near the telephone.
3. Locate sources of assistance with medical problems.	• Class discusses the availability of medical specialists. • Students play a matching game in which they identify the doctor to use for particular kinds of problems. • Students identify community clinics, hospitals, and agencies that assist citizens. • An online resource is http://kidshealth.org/parent/firstaid_safe/. This site has categorical information available for parents, children, and teens.	• Doctor or nurse discusses medications available for home use and the importance of taking prescribed dosages of medication. • Local druggist discusses the functions of home medications. • Parents show students what medications are kept in the home. • Parents discuss with student the labels found on medicine bottles in the home. • Parents discuss with the student the common medicines found in their home and their appropriate uses. • Pharmacist discusses the use of various medicines for minor illnesses and accident. • Class discusses first aid techniques. The following website has first aid information for many ailments and emergencies: http://www.mayoclinic.com/health/firstaidindex/firstaidindex.

DAILY LIVING SKILLS

Objectives	Activities/Strategies	Adult/Peer Roles
4. Identify dosage information from a medicine bottle label.	• Students take a field trip to a drug store. • Class discusses the information written on prescription labels. • Class discusses the differences between prescription and nonprescription medications. • Class discusses common terms used on prescription labels (i.e., tablespoon-tbls., teaspoon-tsp, daily, etc.). • Class brings several empty medicine containers to school and discusses the meanings of the labels. • Class makes up their own prescription labels and places them on the empty medicine containers. • Class discusses the precautions listed on medicine bottle and the importance of taking the prescribed dosages.	• Nurse or paramedic demonstrates first aid. • Members of emergency medical technicians present their equipment and methods and discuss their training. • Red Cross training course is delivered by certified instructor. • Parents practice first aid techniques with the student at home.
5. List common medicines found in the home and their uses.	• Class lists on chalkboard the common medicines their families keep in the home and identify one use for each medication. • Students construct a bulletin board of over-the-counter medicines that should be kept in their homes for minor illnesses and accidents. • Class role-plays contracting minor illnesses and accidents and the prescription of the appropriate medication.	

Domain: Daily Living Skills
Competency: 3. Caring for Personal Needs
Subcompetency: 16. Practice Personal Safety

Objectives	Activities/Strategies	Adult/Peer Roles
1. Identify ways to secure home from intruders.	• Students discuss the purpose of securing one's home from intruders. • Students discuss methods of securing their home from intruders. • Students discuss other ways to deter intruders (pets, burglar alarms). • Class lists on chalkboard the ways to secure home from intruders.	• Parents discuss with student the risks involved in not securing one's home. • Parents and student discuss methods used in the home to secure home from intruders. • Neighborhood watch groups discuss the purpose and methods of home security. • Police officer explains techniques to secure home from intruders.
2. Identify things to do to avoid personal assault.	• Students define personal assault. • Class lists on chalkboard the activities which increase the chances of personal assault (hitchhiking, walking alone late at night, etc.). • Class lists on the chalkboard activities that reduce the possibility of assault (walking with a friend, carrying pocket change for telephone calls in case of emergency, parking your car in lighted areas at night, etc.). • Students role-play an assault situation and discuss what could have been done to avoid the situation.	• Parents discuss with student ways that people can be assaulted in the neighborhood. • Parents discuss precautionary measures they take to prevent assault. • Parents and student visit with law enforcement agency concerning techniques to avoid assault. • Parents and student visit a self-defense school. • Self-defense representative demonstrates self-defense to students. • Law enforcement officer discusses ways to avoid personal assault.
3. Identify and demonstrate self-protection or self-defense behaviors and techniques.	• Self-defense instructor discusses and demonstrates self-protection and self-defense behaviors. • Students discuss protection and defense concepts, and, with approval and instruction, practice self-defense behaviors with self-defense instructor. • Class discusses the importance of cyber safety and ways to protect identity. The following website offers suggestions on internet safety and security: http://kidshealth.org/teen/safety/safebasics/internet_safety.html. An additional resource for online personal safety that can be downloaded and printed: http://isafe.org/xblock/docs/Online_Personal_Safety_Tip_Sheet.pdf.	• Parents demonstrate to student how they believe they would defend themselves. • Parents and students visit self-defense school. • Self-defense instructor demonstrates self-defense and self-protection behaviors. • Parents point out poisonous substances in the home. • Paramedics discuss poisonous hazards and individual responsibilities.

DAILY LIVING SKILLS

Objectives	Activities/Strategies	Adult/Peer Roles
4. Identify precautions to follow when dealing with strangers.	• Students discuss dos and don'ts when meeting strangers. • Students take turns simulating interactions with strangers and then evaluating each other. • Students discuss what strangers could do to them if they are not cautious. • Students role-play appropriate behaviors upon meeting strangers. • Class lists on chalkboard precautions to follow when dealing with strangers.	• Parents and/or peers discuss the dos and don't's of meeting strangers. • Parents role-play with the student how they behave with strangers.
5. Identify potential safety hazards in the home.	• Students construct posters or a bulletin board with magazine pictures of poisonous substances. • Class discusses the dangers of swallowing these poisonous substances. • Students discuss the significance of locating and checking electrical outlets and cords, gas appliances, and light switches for safety. • Students discuss the dangers of electrical shock. • Students are shown what constitutes a household hazard. • Students maintain a scrapbook of pictures of household hazards. • Students collect a notebook of sources to correct hazards.	• Representatives from the public utilities give home hazard presentations. • Gas company and electrical company representatives give presentation concerning potential utility hazards. • Parents discuss potential hazards in the home (e.g., stairways, electrical outlets, and flammables). • Insurance agent discusses household hazards and means of prevention.
6. List and demonstrate actions to take in the event of an emergency.	• Class discusses first aid techniques. • Techniques for specific emergencies are demonstrated. • Students role-play administering first aid to each other. • Class lists on chalkboard the vital information to be conveyed in emergency situations. • Students simulate emergency procedures at school (e.g., fire, tornado, etc.). • Students take field trip to Red Cross Emergency Center. • Students are shown how to extinguish different types of fires. • Students plan evacuation procedures for given situations (their own house, hypothetical situations, etc.). • Class discusses emergency phone numbers and procedures for summoning emergency assistance.	• Parents practice emergency drills in the home. • Nurse or paramedic demonstrates first aid. • Emergency squad presents its equipment and methods and discusses its training. • Red Cross instructor delivers training course. • Parents practice first aid techniques with the student at home. • Parents identify possible sources of fire in the home, as well as how to prevent and extinguish them. • Parents show the student the best means for exiting various parts of the house in the event of serious fire. • Family practices fire drills. • Parents discuss severe weather conditions and safety procedures.

Domain: Daily Living Skills
Competency: 4. Demonstrating Relationship Responsibilities
Subcompetency: 17. Understanding Relationship Roles and Changes With Friends and Others

Objectives	Activities/Strategies	Adult/Peer Roles
1. Identify reasons for establishing relationships.	• Class discussion focuses on the nature of the various relationships we have with others and ways in which our feelings characterize those relationships (e.g., classmate, lunch table buddy, friend who is in the same club or sport, friend who you want to see every day, friend with whom you share secrets and details of your life).	• Parents monitor and support their child's school and community-based relationships. • Parents utilize varying web-based support materials to keep their teens safe. These resources include: The Partnership at Drugfree.org (http://www.drugfree.org/prevent); and for safety on Facebook (http://www.facebook.com/safety/groups/parents).
2. Identify personal responsibilities in relationships.	• Students explore literature that focuses on friendship as well as other relationships; for examples see: http://www.guardian.co.uk/books/2011/sep/07/top-10-novels-teenage-friendship.	
3. Identify joint responsibility in relationships.	• Students role-play situations in which relationships with friends and others are challenged. For suggestions check this site: http://busyteacher.org/3853-role-play-friendship.html.	
4. Demonstrate effective relationships with friends and others.	• Students reflect on the nature of their relationships with friends and others and decide if and what they need to change; teachers create dialog journals with those students who seek support in creating more satisfactory relationships with peers and others. • Schoolds create mentor systems to students are given an opportunity to develop relationships with adults in the building or community.	

Domain: Daily Living Skills
Competency: 4. Demonstrating Relationship Responsibilities
Subcompetency: 18. Understanding Relationship Roles and Changes Within the Family

Objectives	Activities/Strategies	Adult/Peer Roles
1. Identify reasons for establishing relationships.	• Class discussions focus on changing relationships, i.e., how friendships are getting very important and family relationships, while still important, have changed. Students need to know this is a normal course of development. For more information, check this site: http://kidshealth.org/teen/your_mind/Parents/fight.html.	
2. Identify personal responsibilities in relationships.	• Students discuss and role-play ways to interact with family members while supporting a growing need and desire for autonomy. For suggestions on communication skills that support families with growing teens: http://ag.udel.edu/extension/fam/fm/issue/communicationskills.htm.	
3. Identify joint responsibility in relationships.	• Families may need resources navigating teenagers in their homes; for suggestions try: http://www.extension.umn.edu/family/families-with-teens/.	
4. Demonstrate effective relationships with families.	• Class discusses situations in which teens become romantically involved and the mutual responsibilities important in mature relationships. For suggestions: http://www.plannedparenthood.org/health-topics/relationships/safe-your-relationship-19917.htm.	
5. Identify changes when a child enters the family.	• For additional resources for young adults and parents negotiating roles and relationships, the Women's Health Network provides a guide for young adults on their relationships with parents (http://www.cyh.com/HealthTopics/HealthTopicDetails.aspx?p=240&np=296&id=2073) and for parents of young adults (http://youngadults.about.com/od/quarterlife/u/20somethingtab.htm)	
6. Identify common family challenges and a positive way of meeting those challenges.		

Domain: Daily Living Skills
Competency: 4. Demonstrating Relationship Responsibilities
Subcompetency: 19. Demonstrate Care of Children

Objectives	Activities/Strategies	Adult/Peer Roles
1. List the physical and psychological responsibilities involved in child care.	• Class lists on chalkboard the responsibilities in raising children. • Students role-play a family situation with a child, which includes diapering, feeding, stimulation, etc. • Class discusses economic responsibilities of family life. • Class discusses the importance of prenatal care and nutrition.	• Parents identify their responsibilities for maintaining the welfare of children. • Parents assist student in identifying those occasions in which children need assistance from older family members. • Staff from child care center explains physical responsibilities involved in child care.
2. Identify basic stages of child development and a characteristic of each.	• Students observe pictures of children at different developmental levels (infant, toddler, preschool, school age, etc.), and list notable characteristics of children at those levels. • Students go on a field trip to a day-care center, nursery school, Head Start, or public school to observe levels of development. • Class discusses physical growth and development skills. • Class discusses appropriate growth for young children. • Class lists on chalkboard the basic stages of child development.	• Personnel from day-care center discuss growth and development of a child and the impact on the family. • Parents discuss the student's own growth sequence, using photographs of the student at different levels. • Parents encourage the student to observe a child's development.

DAILY LIVING SKILLS

Objectives	Activities/Strategies	Adult/Peer Roles
3. Identify potential dangers and required safety measures.	• Class identifies poisons found in the home. • Class discusses safety hazards for children in the home (e.g., medicine bottles, razor blades, detergent, etc.). The following website has a PDF checklist on child safety in the home: http://www.extension.iastate.edu/Publications/PM1621.pdf/ • Student role-plays emergency situation and procedures for a child who has ingested poison or has been cut severely. • Class lists on chalkboard the emergency procedures for a child who has ingested poison or has been cut severely. • Class discusses obtaining emergency assistance for a child who has ingested poison or has been cut severely. • Students construct a computer-based presentation on various poisons and immediate treatments for children. For information, the following website is helpful: http://pediatrics.aappublications.org/content/112/5/1182.full. Also, students should know the national hotline phone number for poison control centers in the United States: 1-800-222-1222. • Class discusses several outside-the-home dangers to children, such as playing with matches, playing in hazardous areas, becoming friendly with strangers, accepting candy or rides from strangers. • Students identify community sources that can assist parents with hazardous conditions or situations. • Class lists, on the chalkboard or newsprint, potential dangers to children outside the home.	• Parents instruct the student in the proper storage of poisonous substances, medications, and sharp objects. • Parents discuss with student the measures they take when a child ingests poison or is cut severely. • Nurse or paramedic demonstrates immediate first aid for a child who has ingested poison or has been cut severely. • Parents show the student proper methods of feeding, changing, and bathing young children. • Other adults with children encourage the student to observe how they perform certain aspects of child rearing (e.g., breastfeeding, infant stimulation, sickness prevention, etc.). • Parents discuss with students safety precautions to take when playing outdoors. • Members of several community agencies (police, fire protection, animal control) discuss hazards and ways to prevent them.
4. Demonstrate procedures for care of a child's physical health and identify common childhood illnesses, symptoms, and treatment.	• Students construct a "symptom chart" for each common disease. • Class lists on chalkboard the common childhood illnesses and the symptoms they experienced. • Students practice using thermometers, vaporizers, etc. • Class discusses disease prevention techniques in the home. • Students construct a baby health bulletin board.	• Pediatrician or nurse discusses childhood illnesses. • Nurse assists students in solving hypothetical child health problems. Nursery personnel describe their methods, experiences, and training.

Objectives	Activities/Strategies	Adult/Peer Roles
5. Identify parental responsibilities involved in the psychological care of the child.	• Students are given a demonstration of prenatal care: medical checkups, proper diet. • Students go on a field trip to a nursery to observe children and techniques of child care. • Basic toilet training techniques are demonstrated. • Students perform proper infant stimulation exercises and identify the reasons for such activities. • Students go on a field trip to a supermarket to select items suitable for infant or child diet. • Proper methods of physically handling infants and children are demonstrated. • Students select appropriate clothing for children relative to the seasons. • Class discusses the need for regular medical checkups for children. • Students practice bathing an infant or child, using a doll in a bassinet or tub. • Class discusses the advantages of breastfeeding and bottle-feeding for infants.	• Pediatrician or nurse from baby clinic discusses ways to enhance child's well being through proper care. • Parents allow the student to assist in taking care of younger family members. • Parents show the student proper methods of feeding, changing, and bathing young children. • Other adults with children encourage the student to observe how they perform certain aspects of child-rearing (e.g., breastfeeding, infant stimulation, sickness prevention, etc.).

Domain: Daily Living Skills
Competency: 5. Buying, Preparing, and Consuming Food
Subcompetency: 20. Plan and Eat Balanced Meals

Objectives	Activities/Strategies	Adult/Peer Roles
1. List the basic food groups required in each meal.	• Class discussion will focus on ways to incorporate each food group into each meal. Students will create a series of meal posters that have food group options. For more information check this site: http://www.livestrong.com/article/345768-meals-that-include-all-food-groups/.	
2. Identify appropriate foods eaten at typical daily meals.	• Students will research ways to include appropriate food into typical daily meals. The Center for Disease Control has suggested guidelines: http://www.cdc.gov/nutrition/everyone/basics/foodgroups.html.	

DAILY LIVING SKILLS

Objectives	Activities/Strategies	Adult/Peer Roles
3. Plan a day's balanced meals within a given budget.	• Since it can be frustrating trying to eat healthy and maintain a strict budget for food, a website developed by the USDA has done some of the work: http://www.choosemyplate.gov/healthy-eating-on-budget.html • Students can use the website: http://www.foodonthetable.com/ for meal planning down to specific ingredients and stores in which to buy the products. Students can design menus, find out best places in their communities to shop for ingredients, and get step-by-step directions for meal preparation. • Students will describe ways their families have made changes in meal planning as a result of their input learned in class. • Families will involve students in meal planning at periodic times throughout the week; students will report their meal planning nutrition and budget to the rest of the class. • As a class project, students will create daily menus with nutrition and budget based on their experimentation in school and at home which they'll compile into a student "cookbook" for publication.	

Domain: Daily Living Skills
Competency: 5. Buying, Preparing, and Consuming Food
Subcompetency: 21. Purchase Food

Objectives	Activities/Strategies	Adult/Peer Roles
1. Create a weekly shopping list and purchase within a budget.	• Class discusses organizing a shopping list (e.g., weekly essentials, milk, eggs, meat, etc.). • Class lists meats by generic names (beef, poultry, fish, pork, etc.). • Teacher demonstrates constructing a weekly shopping list within a given budget. • Class lists a weekly shopping list on chalkboard. • Students practice making an actual list and discuss their rationale with other students. • Students pretend to buy listed items, based on a given amount of money. • Students develop weekly shopping lists, and on a community-based instruction trip to a grocery store indicate the prices of the items on their lists.	• Parents explain their shopping list for the week. • Student takes part in actual construction of the list. • Peers or young adults discuss their experience with using a budget. • Parents discuss their weekly budget with the student. • Home economist explains the importance of developing a weekly shopping list within her budget. • Parents and student go on shopping trips to select fruits, vegetables, meats, etc.
2. List characteristics of perishable foods.	• Teacher demonstrates what to look for when purchasing meat, dairy products, vegetables, etc. • Class discusses seasonal foods and the economics of purchasing them. • Class discusses the expiration dates on perishables (e.g., milk, bread, etc.) in grocery stores. • Students are shown how to determine freshness in fruits, vegetables, breads, meats, etc. • Class lists perishable foods on the chalkboard. • On a community-based instruction trip, students will visit a grocery store to identify perishable foods.	• Parents and student discuss seasonal foods and expiration dates. • Parents allow the student to select foods. • Produce or meat department managers of grocery stores discuss quality of perishable foods.

Objectives	Activities/Strategies	Adult/Peer Roles
3. Identify types and cuts of meat, fish, poultry, and vegetarian proteins.	• Students are shown the kinds of meat and fish, and the ways to identify different cuts of meat, cost of different cuts, etc. • Students discuss chart from grocery store meat department that displays different cuts of meat and fish. • On a community-based instruction trip, students will visit a meat- or fish-packing plant or to a market to examine the types and sizes of cuts. • Students compare nutritional values and costs of various types and cuts of meats (e.g., a roast is as nutritional as a steak but is less costly per pound). • Class lists on chalkboard different types of meat, fish, and poultry.	• Parents discuss different kinds of meat and fish they commonly purchase, including price, cuts, and amount required per person. • Parents help the student identify different cuts of meats through pictures in cookbooks and magazines. Butcher discusses meats, fish, materials, and training.
4. Identify how to use ads and coupons to take advantage of sales.	• Class discusses the pros and cons of taking advantage of specials and stores that offer specials. • Students get ads and role-play items for purchase. • Students take field trip to grocery stores to compare regular and sale-priced items. • Students discuss why they would or would not shop at each of the stores.	• Parents explain the use of newspaper ads to select items for weekly purchases. • Representative of consumer products discusses reading food ads. • Students accompanies parents on grocery shopping trips to help identify sale and nonsale items.

Domain: Daily Living Skills
Competency: 5. Buying, Preparing, and Consuming Food
Subcompetency: 22. Store Food

Objectives	Activities/Strategies	Adult/Peer Roles
1. Identify the need for proper food storage.	• Students discuss the reasons for food storage (e.g., spoilage, disease, bugs, etc.). • Students are shown pictures or other demonstrations of what happens to food that is improperly stored. For an interactive quiz on kitchen food safety (http://homefoodsafety.org/quiz). • Students discuss the consequences of eating spoiled food. • Classroom bulletin board or computer-based presentation that illustrates food storage. • Class lists on chalkboard the reasons for proper food storage.	• Parents explain to the student the reasons that some foods need refrigeration or storage. • Personnel from a food packaging firm discuss the reasons for proper storage of food.

Objectives	Activities/Strategies	Adult/Peer Roles
2. Identify and demonstrate appropriate food storage.	• Teacher identifies the proper methods for storing food (e.g., wrapping, refrigeration, freezer, etc.). • Students identify the location of food storage. • Students discuss the length of time for storage of food before consumption. • Students construct bulletin board illustrating proper methods of food storage. For specific suggestions the following website, Women's and Child's Health Network, is useful (http://www.cyh.com/HealthTopics/HealthTopicDetailsKids.aspx?p=335&np=288&id=1685). • Class lists on chalkboard foods that require storage and the techniques for storage. • Students take a field trip to a food package and storage firm.	• Parents demonstrate proper methods for storing different kinds of food. • Parents discuss how long different kinds of foods may be safely stored. • Personnel who work in food packaging and storage discuss methods of training. • Parents explain different ways in which food can be spoiled.
3. Identify the appearance of foods when they have spoiled.	• Teacher demonstrates different ways to identify spoiled foods (e.g., smell, appearance, taste, etc.). • Students participate in an exercise that asks them to identify spoiled foods. • Students construct bulletin board depicting different types of food spoilage. • Class lists food spoilage indicators on chalkboard. • Students discuss foods that need to be stored. • Students demonstrate the proper food storage procedures for such items as eggs, meat, vegetables, cereals, cakes. • Class lists food storage procedures on chalkboard.	• Parents discuss different ways to identify spoiled foods. • Nurse or paramedic demonstrates the dangers of spoiled foods, ways to identify them, and treatment in case one has eaten spoiled food. • Parents demonstrate appropriate food storage procedures daily. • Parents assist the student in practicing appropriate food storage procedures. • Cafeteria supervisor discusses proper storage.

Domain: Daily Living Skills
Competency: 5. Buying, Preparing, and Consuming Food
Subcompetency: 23. Clean Food Preparation Areas

DAILY LIVING SKILLS

Objectives	Activities/Strategies	Adult/Peer Roles
1. Identify the importance of personal hygiene in food preparation areas.	• Students discuss reasons for personal cleanliness when around areas where food is prepared. • Students discuss the importance of keeping hands clean and wearing a hairnet or hat when handling food. • Students discuss diseases resulting from contamination of food and poor sanitary conditions. • Students take a field trip to a place where food is prepared to hear firsthand the importance of personal hygiene (e.g., hospital cafeteria, restaurant kitchen). • Class lists on chalkboard the reasons for good personal hygiene in food preparation areas.	• Parents stress personal hygiene when preparing meals • County health inspector speaks to class on personal hygiene and food preparation.
2. List reasons for cleaning work area and materials after food preparation.	• Class discusses the reasons for cleaning up immediately after a meal (e.g., neatness, cleanliness, health). • Class discusses proper step-by-step procedures involved in clean-up (e.g., wrapping and storing leftovers, clearing table, scraping plates, etc.). • Class lists on chalkboard the reasons for cleaning work area and materials after food preparation.	• Parents explain after-meal clean-up procedures. • Parents involve student in the actual cleanup process. • Counter personnel or bus boys discuss clean-up procedures.
3. Identify and demonstrate appropriate cleaning procedures.	• Students are shown the procedures used to clean the work area and appliances used in food preparation (e.g., store, kitchen sink, kitchen table, refrigerator, counters, etc.). • Class discusses the type of cleaners (e.g., steel wool, cloths, cleansers, dish soap, etc.) to be used for each job. • Class discusses how often different clean-up jobs must be performed (e.g., daily, weekly, etc.). • Students go on field trip to a cafeteria or restaurant to observe kitchen procedures. • Appropriate cleaning materials are displayed in the class. • Class lists appropriate cleaning procedures on the chalkboard.	• Parents demonstrate proper procedures for cleaning work areas and appliances. • Parents include the student in actual cleanup procedures. • Kitchen personnel of cafeteria or restaurant demonstrate procedures, materials, and appliances.

Objectives	Activities/Strategies	Adult/Peer Roles
4. Identify and demonstrate appropriate waste disposal procedures.	• Students discuss materials to be placed in garbage or disposal unit and proper placement in trash cans. • Students discuss how to set out garbage cans for trash pick-up. • Students discuss the consequences of neglect of waste or improper disposal of waste. • Students take part in trash removal and garbage disposal in home economics class or cafeteria. • Class lists on chalkboard the appropriate waste disposal procedures.	• Parents explain to the student how, when, and where to remove different kinds of trash. • Student is given the responsibility of disposing of waste in the appropriate receptacles after meals. • Sanitation personnel discuss proper preparation of trash, as well as their job duties and preparation.

Domain: Daily Living Skills
Competency: 5. Buying, Preparing, and Consuming Food
Subcompetency: 24. Preparing Meals and Cleaning Up After Dining

Objectives	Activities/Strategies	Adult/Peer Roles
1. Identify food preparation procedures.	• Students are given demonstrations of the preparation of vegetables, meats, fruits, etc. • Students are given demonstrations of the different methods of cooking (e.g., boiling, baking, frying, etc.). • Students take part in actual food preparation. • Students go on a field trip to a school or community kitchen to observe cooking methods. • Students discuss which techniques to use for which foods and why (e.g., frying is faster but adds calories). • Students discuss the importance of proper food preparation techniques (e.g., undercooking or overcooking foods is nutritionally improper). • Class lists on chalkboard the procedures for several food preparation techniques.	• Parents and/or peers demonstrate the preparation of different foods. • Cook demonstrates basic techniques in food preparation.
2. Identify and demonstrate the use of basic appliances and tools.	• Students list kitchen appliances and utensils found in their homes. • Kitchen appliances and utensils and their use are demonstrated. • Students role-play preparation of meals and decide which appliances or utensils to use. • Bulletin board contains pictures of appliances and utensils. • Students go on field trip to the school kitchen. • Class lists on chalkboard the basic appliances and utensils and their uses.	• Parents demonstrate the appliances and utensils in their kitchens. • Cook demonstrates utensils and appliances found in cafeteria or restaurant.

Objectives	Activities/Strategies	Adult/Peer Roles
3. List basic recipe abbreviations and cooking terms.	• Students discuss basic terms such as baste, simmer, marinate, measure, cup, pound, tablespoon, etc., and their abbreviations. • Students discuss wall chart illustrating measures with representative pictures. • Teacher and class demonstrate the basic terms. • Students make flashcards to identify knowledge of food preparation. • Students measure different quantities of liquids and solids. • Teacher demonstrates the use of a recipe card or cookbook in preparing meals. • Students collect recipes from local media and place on bulletin board. • Students follow a set of written instructions in preparing or pretending to prepare a meal. • Class lists on chalkboard the basic recipe abbreviations and cooking terms.	• Parents and/or peers identify terms used in cookbooks and ensure that the students understand what they mean (e.g., baste, simmer, measure, fill, tsp, tbsp, etc.). • Parents or peers demonstrate liquid and solid measures in the kitchen. • Parents encourage the student to do the measuring during actual meal preparation. • Parents or peers demonstrate simple directions in a cookbook or recipe. • Cook discusses the use of recipes.
4. Practice kitchen safety procedures.	• Students compile a scrapbook of the various kitchen hazards and emergencies. • Class discusses safety procedures in food preparation (knife handling, electrical appliance use, turning pot handle to rear of stove, etc.). • Students are shown simple first aid for minor burns. • Students role-play receiving minor burns and applying simple first aid procedures. • Teacher demonstrates how to avoid kitchen fires and how to extinguish different types of fires. • Class lists on chalkboard several kitchen safety procedures.	• Nurse or paramedic discusses first aid for minor burns. • Parents demonstrate for the student the hazards that are present in the kitchen, how accidents can happen, and what to do when they happen.
5. Prepare a full-course meal for one or more people.	• Prepare a complete meal for one or more people. • Students are given a demonstration of the preparation of an entire meal. • Students construct a cookbook of favorite meals.	• Parents involve the student in actual food preparation and meal planning. • Parents allow the student to plan and prepare simple meals on a regular basis.
6. Cleaning up and doing the dishes after dining.		• Parents encourage dishwashing at home on a regular basis. • Students learn proper ways of cleaning dishes whether using a dishwasher: http://www.wikihow.com/Conserve-Water-when-Doing-Dishes Or by hand: http://housekeeping.about.com/od/dishes/ht/dishwashingstep.htm

Domain: Daily Living Skills
Competency: 5. Buying, Preparing, and Consuming Food
Subcompetency: 25. Demonstrate Appropriate Eating Habits

Objectives	Activities/Strategies	Adult/Peer Roles
1. Identify and demonstrate the proper way to set a table and serve food.	• Class discusses why one should display proper eating behaviors. • Proper etiquette and eating behavior are demonstrated (e.g., requesting food, proper use of utensils, placement of napkin, etc.). • Students role-play eating a meal using proper etiquette. • Utilizing community-based instruction, students visit both fast food and sit-down dining restaurants to practice etiquette. • Class lists on chalkboard the reasons for proper manners and eating behaviors.	• Parents explain their understanding of proper table manners. • Parents demonstrate proper table manners and use of utensils.
2. Identify the need for proper manners and eating behavior.	• Students are instructed in the proper way to eat a meal (e.g., how to cut meat, serve oneself, pass food, request seconds, etc.). • Students role-play eating a meal. • Students discuss the most and least difficult areas of etiquette experienced during role-playing. • Students design an evaluation checklist of etiquette to be adhered to during meals. • Students eat a meal while being videotaped (tape could be used to correct errors). • Students take a field trip to a local restaurant, eat a meal, and critique each other using guidelines for evaluation designed by the class.	• Parents develop a hierarchy of eating skills and manners for the student; the hierarchy could be used as a checklist of which skills the student already has and which skills he or she needs. • Home economist works with the student and parents on identifying and developing appropriate eating skills.

Objectives	Activities/Strategies	Adult/Peer Roles
3. Identify and demonstrate proper manners and eating behavior at home or in the community.	• Students are shown the proper methods of setting a table and serving different types of food (e.g., use of hot pads, appropriate serving dishes, how to carve different meats, etc.). • Students role-play setting the table and serving foods. • Class lists the process for setting a table and serving food. • Class lists on chalkboard the dos and don'ts of eating at a restaurant (e.g., reading a menu, ordering, tipping, etc.). • Students role-play eating in a restaurant in class. • Class tours different types of restaurants. • Class discusses the prices and kinds of foods served at different types of restaurants. • Class takes a field trip to eat at a local restaurant.	• Parents and/or peers demonstrate the proper methods of setting the table. • Parents and/or peers demonstrate the proper way to serve foods. • Parents involve the student in setting the table and serving meals at home. • Home economist demonstrates serving food. • Parents discuss with student the proper manners to display when dining out. • Parents have the student accompany them when they dine out. • Parents monitor the student's behavior in this situation and correct inappropriate behaviors. • Head waiter discusses the dos and don't's of dining out.

Domain: Daily Living Skills
Competency: 6. Buying and Caring for Clothing
Subcompetency: 26. Wash/Clean Clothing

Objectives	Activities/Strategies	Adult/Peer Roles
1. Identify the following laundry products and their uses: bleaches, detergents, and fabric softeners.	• Students bring to school magazine pictures of laundry products for a collage. • Teacher demonstrates the major types of laundry products by category and brand name (e.g., bleaches, Clorox; detergents, Tide; fabric softeners, Bounce dryer sheets). • Students list on chalkboard which laundry products are used for what purposes. • Demonstrations or films show how each product is best used. • Students role-play choosing the appropriate product for a particular job.	• Parents or peers identify laundry products in their home and how they are used. • Parents allow the student to choose and measure the type of product required for a particular washing.

Objectives	Activities/Strategies	Adult/Peer Roles
2. Identify and demonstrate appropriate laundering procedures for different types of clothing.	• Students discuss washing and drying temperatures recommended for specific fabrics. • Class has demonstrations or films of operating a washer and dryer, hand washing, and removing spots from clothing. The following video provides directions with humor in doing laundry: http://www.dailymotion.com/video/xm77ut_doing-laundry-the-owner-s-manual-of-adulthood_school. • Students participate in the above procedures. • Students list on chalkboard the cleaning techniques for certain fabrics (e.g., dry cleaning for wools, etc.). • Students select appropriate laundering products for particular fabrics. • Students read cleaning labels in clothing and sort clothing by types of cleaning techniques required.	• Parents or peers demonstrate how to perform the various laundering procedures. • Laundering expert demonstrates and explains these procedures.
3. Demonstrate use of laundry facilities at a laundromat.	• Students are given a demonstration of coin-operated washers and dryers. • Students take a field trip to a laundromat for a demonstration of the various machines. • Students wash and dry a load of laundry at a laundromat.	• Parents or peers take the student to a laundromat to do laundry. • Laundromat owner explains the various cleaning services available at his or her establishment.

Domain: Daily Living Skills
Competency: 6. Buying and Caring for Clothing
Subcompetency: 27. Purchase Clothing

Objectives	Activities/Strategies	Adult/Peer Roles
1. List basic articles of clothing.	• Students list on chalkboard all articles of clothing that constitute a basic wardrobe (including optional items). • Students discuss what they would want to include in their basic wardrobe. • Students create a poster or computer-based presentation depicting basic wardrobe items.	• Parents or peers explain articles of clothing that constitute a basic wardrobe. • Parents or peers have the student make up a list of items he or she would like to have in his or her basic wardrobe. • Seamstress or fashion expert demonstrates different articles of clothing required in a basic wardrobe.

DAILY LIVING SKILLS

Objectives	Activities/Strategies	Adult/Peer Roles
2. Identify personal body measurements and clothing sizes.	• Teacher demonstrates how body measurements relate to having clothing fit properly. • Students are shown how to determine if an article of clothing fits properly. • Class discusses how measurements can change with growth and weight loss or weight gain. • Students are shown how to identify clothing tags. • Students make lists on chalkboard of personal clothing sizes.	• Parents or peers demonstrate how to take body measurements. • Parents or peers discuss how body measurements can change. • Parents or peers show how to read clothing labels. • Parents and student take trip to clothing store to examine clothing tags and try on merchandise for proper fitting.
3. List major clothing categories by dress, work, casual, sports, and school.	• Teacher discusses the purpose of each type of clothing and shows pictures of each type. • Students cut out pictures of people wearing different types of clothing for specific activities. • Students discuss why and when to wear each type of clothing. • Students see films of situations for which each type of clothing might be appropriate.	• Parents or peers discuss the different categories of clothing, and why and when each type may be worn. • Parents or peers help the student identify the characteristics of each type of clothing.
4. Given a hypothetical budget, select a school wardrobe.	• Home economics teacher demonstrates construction of a clothing budget. • Students cut out clothing sale ads and put them on the bulletin board. • Students discuss what items of clothing are most essential for their wardrobe (basic clothing items). • Students use mock store and play money to shop for their wardrobes. • Students discuss the economics of clothing purchases (color selection so various articles can be interchanged to make varied outfits). • Teacher discusses ways to identify good workmanship (hence, longer life) of clothing articles.	• Parents explain their clothing budget. • Student accompanies parents or peers on shopping trips. • Parents help the student plan for a shopping trip by making a list of clothing needs. • Parents explain what comparison shopping means and show examples of this during shopping trip. • Student purchases his or her own clothing when accompanied by a parent or peer. • Peers help the student identify clothing sale ads in the newspaper.
5. State the importance of matching colors and fabrics.	• Teacher discusses with student the images conveyed to others due to one's dress or appearance. • Class discusses feelings of mixing plaids with stripes and other combinations. • Class discusses mixing of fabrics (e.g., cotton, wool, silk, etc.).	• Parents or peers discuss with student the importance of appropriate dress as related to one's image and in gaining respect from others. Female students examine a style website and decide their preferred style of clothing: http://fashion.beautyandlace.net/whats-your-dressing-style/ • Another helpful website for matching fabrics with style and season is: http://www.define-your-style-clothes-magic.com/ • Parents assist the student in selecting matching colors and fabrics.

Domain: Daily Living Skills
Competency: 6. Buying and Caring for Clothing
Subcompetency: 28. Iron, Mend, and Store Clothing

Objectives	Activities/Strategies	Adult/Peer Roles
1. Identify and demonstrate proper ironing procedures for common fabrics.	• Teacher demonstrates proper ironing techniques for specific articles of clothing (how to iron shirts, pleats, flatwork, etc.). • Teacher demonstrates what happens to fabric when the wrong temperature is used on fabrics (using fabric scraps). • Students identify fabrics and match with proper ironing temperatures. • Teacher demonstrates the proper method used to iron each type of fabric (e.g., temperature setting, use of starch or sizing, etc.). • Students construct a notebook of different kinds of fabrics and proper methods of ironing. • Students practice ironing different articles of clothing.	• Parents instruct and supervise the student in ironing to ensure proper temperatures are being used. • Someone with expertise in alterations speaks to the class on ironing, including using proper temperatures. • Parents or peers identify different types of fabrics by sight, touch, and labels. • Parents or peers demonstrate proper method of ironing different fabrics. • Student assists parents in ironing.
2. Demonstrate appropriate safety precautions for using ironing equipment.	• Teacher demonstrates the use and the maintenance of a steam iron, dry iron, and aerosol products. • Teacher identifies parts of a steam iron and dry iron. • Students practice using a steam and dry iron. • Students demonstrate storage procedures for ironing equipment and proper use of aerosol products.	• Parents or peers demonstrate the use and maintenance of a steam iron, dry iron, and aerosol products. • Student assists parents in ironing and equipment maintenance.
3. Identify when, how, and where to store clothing.	• Teacher demonstrates the storing of clothing, how it is done, when it should be done, and where clothing should be stored (e.g., how to organize a closet, covering garments in plastic, use of mothballs or cedar chips, etc.). • Students visit firms that store household items, including clothing.	• Parents demonstrate storing clothing. • Worker in storage conducts discussion with students about storing clothes.

DAILY LIVING SKILLS

Objectives	Activities/Strategies	Adult/Peer Roles
4. Identify and demonstrate procedures for mending clothing.	• Teacher demonstrates the use of a needle and thread and a sewing machine to perform mending. • Students practice matching color of thread and cloth, and pinning and basting cloth. • Students discuss the reasons for the techniques. • Students practice various mending chores. • Teacher demonstrates different ways to repair torn fabric including patching. Here is a useful website that has 10 tips for repairing clothing: http://diyfashion.about.com/od/mendingandalterations/tp/Repair_and_Mend_Clothing.htm • Students practice these different methods. • Class discusses the best method of repair for each kind of tear and each fabric.	• Parents or peers demonstrate to the student how to match thread and cloth color and how to pin and baste cloth before sewing. • Seamstress (or parent) demonstrates techniques to the student. • Parents or peers demonstrate hand and machine methods of performing simple mending. • Parents or peers demonstrate different methods of fabric repair to the student. • Seamstress (or parent) demonstrates the different kinds of stitches that can be used to make repairs and emphasizes the best methods of repair for each kind of tear and fabric.

Domain: Daily Living Skills
Competency: 7. Exhibiting Responsible Citizenship
Subcompetency: 29. Demonstrate Knowledge of Civil Rights and Responsibilities

Objectives	Activities/Strategies	Adult/Peer Roles
1. Identify basic civil rights when being questioned by law enforcement officials.	• Class discusses an individual's inalienable rights. • Students work in pairs and list the rights they feel they have. • Students discuss what one should do if arrested. • Teacher provides students with the following information available through the American Civil Liberties Union: http://www.aclu.org/files/kyr/kyr_english.pdf. • Follow-up activities may include role playing situations in which a student is being questioned by a police officer. Strategies should be recorded for future information. • Follow-up activities may include role playing situations in which a student is being questioned by a police officer. Strategies should be recorded for future information. • Utilizing community-based instruction, students visit local police station or state police barracks for discussion of civil rights and responsibilities of every individual as an adult citizen.	• Parents discuss the importance of knowing basic rights. • Parents point out citizens' rights that are discussed in newspapers, magazines, and news programs. • Law enforcement official or a member of the American Civil Liberties Union discusses a citizen's rights if he or she is arrested.

Objectives	Activities/Strategies	Adult/Peer Roles
2. Locate resources where one can acquire legal aid. For a national resource that provides links to each state use the following online resource: http://www.lawhelp.org.	• Teacher presents resources for legal aid (e.g., United Way Community Directory). • Class works as a unit to locate places where students can receive legal aid starting with this website: http://www.legal-aid.org/en/home.aspx. • Class discusses the role of a lawyer in legal situations.	• Parents discuss where they have received legal assistance. • Speaker from legal aid society presents resources for assistance.
3. Identify actions to take when a crime has been witnessed.	• Class discusses whether or not one should speak to authorities when he or she witnesses a crime. • Class takes a field trip to a police station to discuss citizen action to take when a crime has been committed. • Students collect articles that report cases in which citizens took responsible action.	• Lawyer discusses how to fulfill citizen obligations in specific situations. • Parents model responsible behavior under the law. • Law enforcement official discusses and demonstrates the appropriate report of a crime.
4. List basic civil rights.	• Teacher lists on chalkboard our basic constitutional rights. • Students role-play a citizen being denied his or her basic rights. • Students discuss specific rights in the Bill of Rights and what they understand about them.	• Representatives from American Civil Liberties Union discuss student's rights. • Historian or constitutional law instructor discusses civil rights.
5. Identify who must register with the Selective Service.	• Students discuss the current draft policy and the prior draft policy. • Students discuss the rationale for the draft and express their opinions concerning conditions for being drafted. • Students discuss the possibility of females being drafted in the future. • Students take field trip to local Selective Service office.	• Recruiter speaks to the class regarding the current status of the Selective Service, future possibilities, and the role of inductees at present. • Parents and/or peers discuss their military experiences with the student.
6. Identify when eligible individuals must register.	• Teacher explains intent of potential draftees registering when they become of age. • Students debate the age of potential draftees in reference to the teacher's explanation of intent.	• Recruiter speaks to the class regarding their need to register with the Selective Service when they become of age (18 years old).
7. Locate the address of the Selective Service or recruitment office nearest the student's home.	• Students look in the telephone book for local Selective Service offices and write their addresses on chalkboard. • Students use information from the local armed forces recruiter to locate Selective Service or recruiting offices.	• Parents and student locate the address of the Selective Service offices in the telephone book.

DAILY LIVING SKILLS

Domain: Daily Living Skills
Competency: 7. Exhibiting Responsible Citizenship
Subcompetency: 30. Know Nature of Local, State, and Federal Governments

Objectives	Activities/Strategies	Adult/Peer Roles
1. Identify the purpose of government.	• Teacher explains the purpose of government. • Teachers and students explore the following website, clicking on the appropriate grade level for learners: http://bensguide.gpo.gov/. • Students discuss the influence or role of government in their daily lives (e.g., regulate quality of food and drugs). • Students discuss areas of their lives in which they believe government should not be influential (e.g., religious affiliation, etc.). • Class create word splash or word wall of terms representative of government.	• Parents or peers discuss their understanding of the purpose of the government. • Parents or peers encourage the student to read or watch the news. • Parents or peers discuss the student's understanding of news events related to government.
2. Define democracy and representative government.	• Teacher presents the concepts of democracy and representative government. • Class discusses the way these principles affect us. • Class conducts democratic election of a president and other officers. • Students visit government offices. • Students visit local postal system as an example of government service. • Class talks with members of the student council.	• Elected official or civil servant presents examples of the principles of democracy and representative government. • Instructor in government law makes presentation to class.
3. Identify the branches of government, their functions, and one major official of each branch of government.	• Teacher describes and lists on chalkboard the three branches of government. • Class discusses the functions of the three branches of government. • Class identifies titles of government officials in each branch of government. • Class constructs a bulletin board which represents the responsibilities of each branch. • Students collect news articles about the different branches of government. • Students take a field trip to a court and a legislative body.	• Elected official or civil servant presents the organization and functions of government.

Objectives	Activities/Strategies	Adult/Peer Roles
4. Identify one way states might be different without a federal government.	• Class discusses the Constitution and the Declaration of Independence. • Teacher places reproductions of the documents on the bulletin board. • Class discusses how these documents affect us. • Class discusses the purposes of the federal government (e.g., provide money to states for support services, building maintenance; pass laws, etc.). • Class discusses what the states would be like without a federal government.	• Parents buy reproductions of the Constitution and the Declaration of Independence and read them through with the student. • Parents discuss with student the capacity and function of federal government.
5. Identify one duty of each level of government.	• Students identify the three levels of government (local, state, and federal) and write them on the chalkboard. • Students discuss the differences between the levels of government and list them on the chalkboard. • Class takes field trips to local, state, and federal offices for tours and presentations. • Class discusses responsibilities of each level of government and effects upon us (i.e., housing, taxes, building and construction, public schools, etc.).	• Parents discuss with student the differences and responsibilities of the three levels of government. • Local law instructor discusses levels of government with class.

Domain: Daily Living Skills
Competency: 7. Exhibiting Responsible Citizenship
Subcompetency: 31. Demonstrate Knowledge of the Law and Ability to Follow the Law

Objectives	Activities/Strategies	Adult/Peer Roles
1. List types of local laws.	• Teacher describes and gives examples of local laws which students should be familiar with (e.g., property, traffic, etc.). • Students list on chalkboard examples of reasons such local laws are needed. • Students role-play a situation in which such laws are heeded or abused.	• Parents emphasize the importance of local laws. • Police officer speaks on the importance of local laws.
2. Identify possible consequences of violating laws.	• Teacher describes and lists on the chalkboard the penalties for breaking different laws. • Students work in pairs and list all possible penalties. • Students construct a bulletin board which illustrates several major infractions and their penalties. • Students discuss appropriateness of consequences for infractions of laws and offer alternative suggestions.	• Parents or peers explain why it is necessary to obey laws. • Lawyer, judge, or law enforcement officer talks about the penalties for breaking different laws.
3. List basic reasons for government and laws.	• Class discusses the function of laws. • Class discusses the distinction between government and laws. • Students go to a meeting of an elected body in session. • Teacher discusses basic laws.	• Parents or peers explain the reasons for a law and how it affects them. • Parents or peers discuss how laws change. • Lawyer, judge, or law enforcement officer discusses the basic ideas of law.
4. Explain and demonstrate the basic court system and its procedures.	• Teacher discusses the basic court procedures. • Class discusses the hierarchy of courts in the state-federal system. • Class discusses settling a dispute outside of court. • Students visit a court in session. • Class conducts a mock trial. • Class discusses trial by jury or judge. • Class discusses the appeal process. • Class discusses the function of local courts in relation to everyday living.	• Parents take the student to see a court proceeding. • A judge or lawyer explains the court system.

Domain: Daily Living Skills
Competency: 7. Exhibiting Responsible Citizenship
Subcompetency: 32. Demonstrate Knowledge of Citizen Rights and Responsibilities

Objectives	Activities/Strategies	Adult/Peer Roles
1. Locate community services available to citizens.	• Class discusses and lists on chalkboard the types of service available in the community. • Students look through the newspaper, listen to radio and television, and record a list of the community services. • Teacher and students work together using the following website to explore social service agencies, their functions, and locations throughout various communities: http://connectyou.org/. • Utilizing community-based instruction, students visit several local service agencies, collect brochures, and interview employees about services they provide. If possible, students digitally tape their interviews and create a computer-based presentation once all information is sorted and summarized. • Students discuss the services they feel are needed.	• Representatives from community services discuss the various services offered. • Parents and the student visit community departments to explore services.
2. List major responsibilities of citizens.	• Students discuss and list on chalkboard what constitutes a "good" citizen. • Students collect articles that represent the responsibilities of citizenship and display them on poster board.	• Parents or peers discuss responsibilities of a citizen. • Parents take the student with them when they vote, pay taxes, attend community meetings, etc. • Local official discusses the rights and responsibilities of a citizen to local government.

DAILY LIVING SKILLS

Objectives	Activities/Strategies	Adult/Peer Roles
3. Identify voting requirements and demonstrate procedures.	• Teacher and students investigate the following website to learn about voting in national, state, and local elections: http://www.usa.gov/Citizen/Topics/Voting.shtml. • Students construct a mock voting booth. • Students display sample ballots on poster board. • Students construct a bulletin board of upcoming elections and pictures of candidates (using newspaper clippings and materials from party headquarters). • Students call or write registrar of voters for information on voting requirements. • Students visit a voting booth on an election day. • Students practice voting with sample ballots and instruction forms. • Students hold a mock election.	• Representatives such as city clerk, registrar of voters, etc., discuss the particular requirements and procedures necessary for voting. • Parents allow the student to accompany them when they go to vote.
4. Identify why it is important to be an informed voter.	• Class discusses the responsibilities of an informed voter. • Students work in pairs and list possible implications surrounding voting choices. • Students collect articles about different candidates and keep a file. • Class discusses propaganda and campaign tactics. • Class discusses all types of elections and the need to be informed (i.e., from local school levy issues to national issues).	• Parents or peers encourage the student to watch news and candidate specials on television. • Parents or peers discuss the stances of candidates and possible implications of their election. • Representatives of the candidates present their positions. • Representatives of the League of Women Voters present information about candidates and issues.
5. List the dates for primary and general elections, and demonstrate procedures for registration.	• Students complete mock registration forms. • Students construct a bulletin board that states necessary steps when registering to vote. • Students discuss voting dates for primary and general elections.	• Parents take the student with them when they go to register to vote. • Registrar of Voters discusses procedures and forms.
6. Identify sources that inform the voter about election issues.	• Students clip articles from newspapers and magazines on election issues. • Students discuss current events which are relevant election issues. • Teacher reads articles aloud to the class. • Teacher lists on chalkboard the pros and cons of an election issue, as students discuss them.	• Parents discuss ways to locate information on election issues. • Organization (e.g., The League of Women Voters) presents information on election issues. • Guest speaker from the League of Women Voters discusses ways to locate information on election issues. • Guest speaker from the local newspaper explains how newspapers obtain information on election issues.

Domain: Daily Living Skills
Competency: 8. Utilizing Recreational Facilities and Engaging in Leisure
Subcompetency: 33. Demonstrate Knowledge of Available Community Resources

Objectives	Activities/Strategies	Adult/Peer Roles
1. List sources of information about specific recreational activities.	• Students compile a listing of recreational activities from newspapers, local magazines, television, online sources, and personal observation. • Students construct a bulletin board depicting the various activities. • Class discusses favorite activities. • Class takes field trips to YMCA/YWCA, community centers, civic center, playground, park, etc. • Different students present the activities available through community agencies. • Students compile a notebook of sources. • Students identify prerequisites of participation (e.g., membership, physical exam, etc.).	• Recreation workers, arts and crafts personnel, YMCA/YWCA personnel, church youth group members, etc., make presentations to the class. • Parents or peers identify preferred community activities.
2. List activities appropriate to each season of the year.	• Students list on chalkboard activities appropriate for each of the four seasons. • Students discuss sports events they participate in and the time of year they participate. • Teacher contacts the local parks and recreation department for a list of seasonal programs.	• Parents encourage the student to participate in individual and group activities. • Local sports announcer discusses seasonal sports activities. • Parents assist the student in enrolling (if necessary) in a fitness program.
3. Locate recreational facilities and equipment in the community.	• Students investigate local recreation department websites for listing of community activities. • Utilizing community-based instruction, students visit recreation facilities in their community and collect schedules, brochures, and other program information. • Students demonstrate the ability to use a facility and equipment (e.g., swimming pool, gymnastic apparatus, etc.) under the supervision of authorized adults. • Students develop a recreational plan suited to their own personal interests and needs. • Fitness expert demonstrates proper use of facilities and equipment. • Students make phone inquiries about availability of various recreational facilities.	• Facility personnel demonstrate proper facility usage. • Parents or peers demonstrate proper techniques for using equipment. • Representative from community parks and recreation department tells students about facilities and opportunities.

DAILY LIVING SKILLS

Objectives	Activities/Strategies	Adult/Peer Roles
4. Participate in recreational activities outside the home.	• Class constructs a large-scale area map indicating the location of all facilities and activities offered. • Students research membership options and/or participate in one or more of the identified activities and organizations. • Students construct bulletin board depicting involvement in community recreation.	• Parents or peers assist the student in finding the location of activities, establishing means of transportation, and engaging in activities. • Recreation personnel give periodic presentations about new programs of activities.

Domain: Daily Living Skills
Competency: 8. Utilizing Recreational Facilities and Engaging in Leisure
Subcompetency: 34. Choose and Plan Activities

Objectives	Activities/Strategies	Adult/Peer Roles
1. List personal leisure activities.	• Students discuss how interest and abilities are a part of deciding favorite activities. • Students list on chalkboard personal leisure activities. • Students discuss differences between leisure and nonleisure activities. • Students make a chart of leisure-time activities. • Students discuss why they have chosen particular activities. • Students participate in new leisure activities.	• Parents or peers help the student evaluate favorite activities. • People with unique recreation interests discuss and demonstrate their experiences with the class (e.g., judo, karate, skydiving, etc.).
2. List costs, times, locations, and physical requirements of activities.	• Class lists on chalkboard the cost, location, and time factors involved in various forms of recreation. • Class discusses the way in which cost, time, and location influence one's choice of activity. • Students collect cost, time, and location factors in a notebook for future reference.	• Parents or peers help the student plan a budget that incorporates recreational expenses. • Parents assist the student in determining the cost of participation in a specific recreational activity including whether a physical or some type of physician approval is needed for the sport or recreation choice. • Representatives of particular activities discuss the costs, time, and location considerations involved in an activity. • Parents or peers assist the student with transportation to and from activities. • Parents assist the student in determining if he or she is physically ready for the recreational activity and if he or she has enough money to participate in the activity.

Objectives	Activities/Strategies	Adult/Peer Roles
3. Develop an individual plan of leisure activities.	• Students choose a common recreational activity, research the cost and physical requirements of that activity, and report findings to the class. These findings from individual students can be summarized into a computer-based presentation and handouts can be made available to class members and families for their information. • Students match on chalkboard physical requirements and financial costs with common recreational activities. • Students list on chalkboard leisure activities, arrangements to be made, and times and days to engage in activities. • Students complete individual plans for a given period of time. • Students can journal their plans and progress.	• Peers and young adults describe their experiences with activities and planning. • Parents assist the student in carrying out activities that student describes in his or her plans.

Domain: Daily Living Skills
Competency: 8. Utilizing Recreational Facilities and Engaging in Leisure
Subcompetency: 35. Demonstrate Knowledge of the Value of Recreation

Objectives	Activities/Strategies	Adult/Peer Roles
1. List differences between leisure that involves nonpaid work activity and relaxation.	• Students define work time on chalkboard. • Students define leisure time and leisure options. • Students demonstrate their hobbies. • Students explore possibilities for hobbies through visits to hobby stores, craft exhibits, sports shows, etc. • Class creates a bulletin board which illustrates various kinds of recreation.	• Local hobby enthusiasts give class displays or demonstrations. • Parents discuss leisure-time activities. • Parents encourage the student to develop specific leisure-time activities that hold the student's interest.
2. List ways in which recreation affects both physical and mental health.	• Class discusses the pleasures of free time. • Class lists on chalkboard indications that there is a need for leisure time (i.e., bored at work, tired, listless, stressed out, etc.). • Class discusses the need for a "time out" recreational period when feeling emotionally and physically stressed. • Class discusses the role of recreation in developing the ability to socialize and work cooperatively with others.	• Parents discuss with the student the value of time away from school or work. • Parents discuss how periods of recreation have a positive bearing upon their emotional and physical functioning. • Parents or peers involve the student in their leisure-time activities.

DAILY LIVING SKILLS

Objectives	Activities/Strategies	Adult/Peer Roles
3. List personal requirements of leisure time.	• Teacher presents on chalkboard daily schedules of certain types of employment. • Students role-play or simulate sedentary employment in the class to compare these activities to leisure-time activities. • Class discusses physical activities which provide physical and emotional change. • Students list on chalkboard the physical activities a person can do independently (bicycling, jogging, swimming, etc.), and the requirements to engage in the activity (i.e., stamina, endurance). • Students explore a variety of hobbies and select one that they can use as a leisure activity. • Class discusses the decisions in selecting activities including leisure that is more sedentary (e.g., video gaming) vs. leisure that is more active (e.g., recreational league sports, walking, jogging, etc.). Further discussion should focus on benefits of active vs. sedentary leisure activities. • Students report on leisure activities.	• Parents discuss options that the student can exercise in leisure time. • Peers and young adults discuss their use of leisure time. • Parents encourage the student to participate in physical activity. • Parents provide opportunities for the student to join in family leisure-time activities. • Parents relate individual and group activities in which they engage.

Domain: Daily Living Skills
Competency: 8. Utilizing Recreational Facilities and Engaging in Leisure
Subcompetency: 36. Engage in Group and Individual Activities

Objectives	Activities/Strategies	Adult/Peer Roles
1. Identify reasons for participating in group activities.	• Students observe several activities involving varying numbers of participants. • Class discusses making friends in a recreational setting. • Class discusses the value of incorporating friends and people with similar interests into recreational activities. • Students participate in a group activity (e.g., softball) and in an individualized activity (e.g., swimming) and compare the two on the chalkboard, with regard to social contact, group support, feelings of belonging, etc. • Class discusses their motivations for participating in group activities, and what they hope to gain.	• Adult participants from several activities discuss advantages and disadvantages, with regard to the number of participants in a group. • YMCA/YWCA member discusses advantages of group activities. • Parents discuss their motivations for participating in group activities. • Parents point out ways in which contact with others leads to increased feelings of competency.

Objectives	Activities/Strategies	Adult/Peer Roles
2. Identify and demonstrate knowledge of rules of group activities.	• Small groups of students learn the rules of different games and activities and explain them to the class. • Class plays the game or activity according to the rules. • Class discusses the necessity of rules in activities and group cooperation. • Each student gets a chance to be "referee" for a game or activity.	• Local umpire, scorekeeper, or referee discusses the reasons for rules in games and activities. • Athletes and coaches discuss abiding by rules. • Parents compare rules for games to other areas of life.
3. List qualities of good sportsmanship.	• Students observe sports events and note instances of good and poor sportsmanship. • Students role-play an activity where participants exhibit good and poor sportsmanship and discuss feelings generated by each. • Class discusses the need for cooperation in recreational activities.	• Athletes discuss their views on what constitutes good sportsmanship. • Coaches discuss the idea that winning isn't everything in activities. • Parents point out how good sportsmanship is similar to group cooperation in the family. • Parents discuss their attitude towards athletes who display poor sportsmanship.
4. Identify and demonstrate the proper care of sports equipment.	• Students visit a local sporting goods store. • Students identify and examine various equipment used in games and activities. • Students are given a demonstration of the maintenance and storage of equipment. • Students bring their sports equipment to class and discuss how they take care of their equipment. • Students are shown the potential safety factors in using equipment. • Fitness expert demonstrates proper use of equipment.	• Personnel of sporting goods store demonstrate the proper use of equipment. • Parents demonstrate proper use of equipment available in the home. • Equipment repairman from local team demonstrates skills and materials.
5. Identify general safety rules of physical activities.	• Class discusses potential dangers of physical activities. • Students discuss activity behaviors that can lead to injuries. • Class discusses rules which prevent potential injuries from occurring.	• Parents discuss with student the purpose of safety rules with activities. • Coach, referee, or athletic director discusses the importance of safety with sports.

DAILY LIVING SKILLS

Domain: Daily Living Skills
Competency: 8. Utilizing Recreational Facilities and Engaging in Leisure
Subcompetency: 37. Plan Recreation and Leisure Activities

Objectives	Activities/Strategies	Adult/Peer Roles
1. Demonstrate knowledge of available community resources.	• Students get travel folders from vacation areas and compare prices. Students can utilize free vacation planning software to help organize vacation plans at: http://www.tripit.com/destinations/vacation-itinerary-template/. • Students list on chalkboard all possible costs in a family vacation. • Class discusses and lists on chalkboard expenditures when vacationing. • Students estimate from mock financial information how much can be spent for a vacation. • Students plan, from mock financial information, a vacation budget. • Teacher discusses vacation possibilities, with regard to the transportation time involved.	• Parents plan vacation activities in the local area for the family. • Representatives from state or local department of parks and recreation discuss a variety of vacation possibilities. • Personnel from the local YMCA/YWCA discuss group vacations.
2. Choose and plan activities.	• Students list on chalkboard the vacation sites available within the local area, in the event of limited time. • Students discuss ways of breaking up blocks of time into smaller vacation periods. • Students discuss what a vacation means to them. • Students construct a vacation and travel bulletin board with information received from vacation sites (e.g., websites, brochures, magazine pictures, travel posters, etc.). • Students plan a mock vacation to a place where they could pursue the activity of their choice (e.g., hiking, swimming, camping, fishing, historical visitations, etc.). • Utilizing community-based instruction, students visit local, state, or regional recreational or historical sites and destinations.	• Parents structure a number of activities for family members. • Travel agent discusses sources of information. • Representative from AAA presents information on planning trips. • Parents plan a family vacation with the student. • Parents allow student to accompany them to local travel agent.

Objectives	Activities/Strategies	Adult/Peer Roles
3. Demonstrate knowledge of the value of recreation.	• Students list on chalkboard the activities that can be done on a day trip. • Students write to state offices to obtain information on recreational opportunities at park facilities.	• Representative from a travel agency lists on chalkboard the approximate expenses of different vacations. • Bank personnel discuss ways to save money for vacation activities. • Parents discuss their vacation expenditures and finances with the student. • Representative from travel agency discusses time as a factor in planning. • Representative from parks and recreation department discusses vacation options that exist in the general area (short-term vacations).
4. Engage in group and individual activities.	• Students collect a notebook with sources of information about vacation spots, agencies, travel routes, estimating costs, etc. • Students take a field trip to the local Chamber of Commerce for resource information. • Students plan a hypothetical trip or summer vacation using websites, brochures, maps, guide books, etc. • Students determine cost, time, transportation, facilities, activities involved, and arrangements to be made for a hypothetical trip. • Students develop a list of local day trip opportunities including recreational, educational or physically strenuous activities (rigorous hiking, biking, running, etc). Students will investigate transportation, fees, and other aspects that must be considered beforehand.	

Objectives	Activities/Strategies	Adult/Peer Roles
5. Adopting and caring for pets.	• Students visit a local humane society or animal shelter to observe the number of unwanted pets in their region. • Utilizing community-based instruction or alternate transportation, students can choose to volunteer time at an animal shelter.	• Class discusses various ways in which pets can be purchased, i.e., pet store, breeder, through want ads or Craigslist, through friends, and animal shelter, etc. Advantages and disadvantages to these various means of acquisition should be highlighted (i.e., puppy mills, overbreeding, etc.). • Many websites offer valuable information about caring for new pets: http://www.ready.gov/animals and help in making decisions about acquiring new pets: http://www.bestfriends.org/theanimals/petcare/

Domain: Daily Living Skills
Competency: 9. Choosing and Accessing Transportation
Subcompetency: 38. Demonstrate Knowledge of Traffic Rules and Safety

Objectives	Activities/Strategies	Adult/Peer Roles
1. Identify the purpose and demonstrate procedures for pedestrian safety signs.	• Students go on a field trip, identify various pedestrian street signs, and describe the significance of each sign. • Students perform various pedestrian procedures and observe others as they do so.	• Police officer discusses and demonstrates procedures when using pedestrian signs, and emphasizes potential consequences of disobedience. • Parents or peers take the student for walks and have him or her point out signs and procedures and demonstrate his or her ability to comply with them.
2. List reasons for common traffic and safety rules and practices.	• Students take a field trip to the traffic control center at the local police department. • Students list on chalkboard the hazards to motorists and pedestrians. • Students discuss the hypothetical situation of a community without traffic or safety rules. • Students relate traffic or safety rules in the community to various rules and procedures in class or school.	• Police officer demonstrates traffic and safety rules. • Parents discuss what happens when people do not obey traffic safety rules.

Objectives	Activities/Strategies	Adult/Peer Roles
3. Identify vehicle safety signs included on the driver's education test.	• Students take a field trip through city to identify the vehicle safety signs and the procedures for conforming to them. • Students construct posters depicting traffic signs. • Teacher quizzes students with the posters. • Students read and discuss appropriate selections from the state driver's license manual regarding traffic signs.	• Parents or peers take the student for rides and point out the signs and procedures necessary for safe travel. • Police officer discusses the necessity of people obeying traffic regulations. • Parents or peers model positive behavior by adhering to rules of the road.

Domain: Daily Living Skills
Competency: 9. Choosing and Accessing Transportation
Subcompetency: 39. Demonstrate Knowledge and Use of Various Means of Transportation

Objectives	Activities/Strategies	Adult/Peer Roles
1. Identify the types of transportation available in the community.	• Class lists on chalkboard the local transportation facilities. • Students take a field trip to local transportation facilities (e.g., taxi stand or office, bus and train stations, airport). • Class constructs a bulletin board of transportation facility locations in their community. The following website might have listings of additional or alternative public transportation options: http://www.publictransportation.org/tools/local/pages/default.aspx. • Class discusses reasons for choosing certain forms of transportation.	• Parents point out all transportation modes available in the student's locality. • Representative operators of transportation discuss their tasks and training.
2. Identify reasons transportation is needed and the type that is most appropriate.	• Students list on chalkboard the types of transportation they use. • Students discuss the best means for transporting themselves to particular places in the community. • Teacher devises hypothetical situations in which students have to find the most appropriate way of getting to particular places.	• Persons who carpool discuss advantages of sharing transportation. • Parents or peers discuss their means of travel to and from work. • Parents assist in identifying the most appropriate ways of travel for their own needs.

Objectives	Activities/Strategies	Adult/Peer Roles
3. Identify and demonstrate procedures to take a train, interstate bus, taxi, and airplane.	• Students buy a bus ticket, deposit it, and take a bus ride. • Students call a taxi, pay the fare, and ride to their destination. • Teacher explains procedures for making flight reservations online, buying tickets, and checking in online, then procedures for getting to the airport in plenty of time for security procedures. The following Transportation Security Website (TSA) can provide answers to many questions about air travel: http://www.tsa.gov/traveler-information. • Students role-play activities relating to transportation.	• Class holds discussion with bus driver, cab driver, train conductor, flight attendant or pilot, and ticket agents from various types of transportation. • Peers accompany the student on various means of transportation.

Domain: Daily Living Skills
Competency: 9. Choosing and Accessing Transportation
Subcompetency: 40. Navigate Local Community

Objectives	Activities/Strategies	Adult/Peer Roles
1. Given a picture of a numbered house, identify numbers of houses on either side.	• Students tour nearby streets to observe the numbering sequence of houses. • Teacher devises a map in which students fill in missing house numbers. • Students find out the addresses of others living on their own street and deduce the way in which their own streets are numbered.	• Parents or peers take the student on a walking tour of neighborhood to identify numbering systems. • City or community planner discusses the overall design for the community.
2. Given city and state maps, identify directions, symbols, and distances.	• Students construct on poster board a large scale localized map or obtain one from the city planning office. • Students study a local street map and then go to the area to investigate it. • Students design a model of a neighborhood, putting in streets, numbers, etc. • Class discusses the necessity of using maps, websites like MapQuest, or Global Positioning Systems (GPS). • Students read state road maps to understand symbols, compute distances, compare time and distance, and describe alternate routes.	• Parents or peers obtain local maps and go over them with the student at home. • Parents or peers take the student in a car and follow the map route while the student observes the map.

Objectives	Activities/Strategies	Adult/Peer Roles
3. Identify basic community resources.	• Students identify signs and symbols that give them direction, information, or guidance in everyday functioning (e.g. crosswalk and street signs).	• Parents and student obtain community directory information from their local mental health association or United Way organization.

Domain: Daily Living Skills
Competency: 9. Choosing and Accessing Transportation
Subcompetency: 41. Understand procedures and processes relating to owning and driving a car

Objectives	Activities/Strategies	Adult/Peer Roles
1. Demonstrate knowledge of appropriate driving techniques for different kinds of driving conditions and problems that could arise because of weather.	• Students list on chalkboard the manual operations and expectations for each weather condition. • Students use driving simulation activities for practice and class discussion. Google Earth offers a driving simulation plug in and the following website has simulations of particular scenarios: http://www.stisimdrive.com/library/videos.html?task=view. • Students list on chalkboard the state laws regarding driving in particular conditions and the necessary vehicular equipment (e.g., snow tires).	
2. Describe appropriate procedures to follow after being involved in an accident.	• Students practice contacting emergency responders, and state and local police. • Teachers review alarming statistics with students regarding cell phones and driving. The following website has specific details: http://www.edgarsnyder.com/car-accident/cell-phone/statistics.html. • Students role-play exchanging information with other drivers and contacting their insurance companies. • Students are shown how to signal other drivers, use danger markers, light flares, etc. • Students go over basic emergency first aid. • Students are instructed about the advantages of having insurance. • Students role-play an accident situation.	• Parents discuss the need for insurance. • Highway patrolman presents procedures to follow in case of an accident. • Local insurance agent discusses car insurance with the class. • Parents discuss with the student what to do in case of an accident.

Objectives	Activities/Strategies	Adult/Peer Roles
3. Identify everyday basic driving knowledge.	• Students participate in driver education classes. • Driving instructors have students practice maneuvers in the parking lot and use simulated driving machines. • Students gain street experience from a licensed adult (teacher, driving instructor, etc.). • Students are given a mock driving test to find their weak areas. • Students role-play driving situations with each other.	• Parents and other adults with licenses take the student out to practice driving skills. • Parents or adults model appropriate driving skills. • Peers relate their experiences with the driving exam.
4. Identify knowledge required for passing the written driver's license exam.	• Teacher uses concepts from a test manual and gives a mock written exam. • Students construct traffic signs and traffic lights from poster board and identify rules. • Students make a game out of holding up traffic signs and identifying the purpose of each sign. • Class goes over the manual in small groups, concentrating on the more difficult aspects of written material. • The following website has some free information on driver's preparation for written and manual tests: http://driversprep.com/.	• Licensing inspectors hold workshop and distribute written information. • Parents go over information with the student at home. • Peers relate their experience pertaining to the written exam.
5. Demonstrate knowledge of basic vehicle maintenance.		
6. Identify documentation required for owning and operating a vehicle.		

SELF-DETERMINATION AND INTERPERSONAL SKILLS

Domain: Self-Determination and Interpersonal Skills
Competency: 10. Understanding Self-Determination
Subcompetency: 42. Understand Personal Responsibility

Objectives	*Activities/Strategies*	*Adult/Peer Roles*
1. To identify areas of personal responsibility.	• The student will write 2 personal goals for each area they are lacking responsibility.	
2. To identify steps to reach personal goals.	• Students will write their future career goal and list the steps needed in order to accomplish or work towards that goal.	
3. To locate items within a grocery store.	• Student will locate various items within a grocery store. These items are things they will be responsible for purchasing when they live on their own: shampoo, deodorant, etc.	
4. To clearly articulate a problem and receive help over the phone.	• Student will pair up with an adult or a peer and do a mock phone call to practice making a phone call for help.	
5. To make a responsible decision based on real-life scenarios.	• Student will be given a list of scenarios that they need to make a responsible decision on.	
6. To recognize/be aware of the consequence of irresponsible choices.	• Student will list times when they weren't responsible and the outcome that occurred because of their decisions.	
7. To recognize the positive effects of responsible choices.	• Student will interview someone in their family (or a friend) in order to discover positive effects related to taking responsibility in their life.	

Domain: Self-Determination
Competency: 10. Understanding Self-Determination
Subcompetency: 43. Identify and Understand Motivation

Objectives	Activities/Strategies	Adult/Peer Roles
1. Identify and describe areas of self-motivation.	• Interview peers (What motivates you?). • Look for motivational quotes in books. • Visit www.inspirational-quotes.info. • Share your favorite motivational quote on a social network, share your feedback with friends.	• Peers will participate in interviews. • Adults will provide access to the internet.
2. List appropriate ways to motivate yourself and others.	• Observe and note examples of when they or others (friends, classmates, teachers, family members) used self-motivation. • Discuss goals with parents/guardian. • Keep a daily journal listing goals, ways to obtain those goals, and positive and negative motivators. • Make a list of rewards and celebrations worth working for. • Break down goals into smaller tasks, reward yourself when goals are met. • Avoid negative people, surround yourself with motivated and positive people. • Exercise, meditate, participate in sports.	• Parents/guardians set up rewards for meeting goals and small celebrations. • Parents/guardians need to provide a positive environment. • Parents/guardians/teachers should provide social rewards such as praise, a nod, or a pat on the shoulder.
3. Identify how motivation affects present and future goal attainment.	• Interview peers (Who is your role-model and why?). • Hang motivational sayings in your locker, in your room, or on your mirror.	

Domain: Self-Determination and Interpersonal Skills
Competency: 10.Understanding Self-Determination
Subcompetency: 44. Anticipate Consequences to Choices

Objectives	*Activities/Strategies*	*Adult/Peer Roles*
1. Describe consequences or outcomes of personal choices.	• Describe consequences or outcomes of personal choices. • Students will explore different stories in the news and the choices and consequences that came of those stories. • Students will read through scenarios and talk through choices that led to that outcome. If the outcome is negative, students will change choices to lead to a positive outcome.	• Students keep a running log at home with their family and/or school with their peers of the consequences they receive, and reflect on why that consequence occurred.
2. List and demonstrate knowledge of ways in which personal choices produce consequences.	• Become aware of the ways personal choices lead to consequences. • Students will explore how consequences came from various choices. • Students will practice making choices that lead to positive consequences.	• Parents help students list possible choices they may make at home or school and the consequences that may occur from them. • Students help their parents create a "fair punishment" list to use at home.
3. Describe the concept of maximum gain for minimum risk in making personal choices.	• Students will learn what it means to have the maximum benefit for minimum risk. • Students will explore different choices and decide the risk that was involved in those choices. • Students will think about where they want to be in adulthood. They will examine how they can make choices of maximum gain to get to that point in life.	• Students discuss with their parents or peers a time when they weighed the risks before making a decision. They then reflect and evaluate if they made the best choice.

SELF-DETERMINATION AND
INTERPERSONAL SKILLS

Domain: Self-Determination and Interpersonal Skills
Competency: 10. Understanding Self-Determination
Subcompetency: 45. Communicate Needs

Objectives	Activities/Strategies	Adult/Peer Roles
1. Identify communication skills necessary in becoming self-determined.	• In small groups, students will develop strategies to successfully express preferred activities in home, school, work, and community settings. • Students will role-play situations in which they use assertive, appropriate language to express their preferences and opinions in school, home, work, and community settings.	• Peers and teachers will provide feedback and suggestions in small group and role-play situations.
2. Demonstrate appropriate communication skills at home, at work, and in the community.	• Students will engage in a number of exercises to assess and improve their listening skills, the foundational skills of successful communication. • Create a listening log to assess at least 6 interactions they've experienced over a 2-day period. No phone conversations, only live! They will record date, time, person with whom they are interacting, and nature of the conversation. Students will note their listening behavior including eye contact, head nodding to indicate interest, asking of questions, and responding to questions asked. Students will analyze their logs to assess their own listening behavior with others.	• Teachers can help the student analyze and assess his or her reflections on his or her listening logs.
3. Identify ways to communicate effectively at home, at work, and in the community.	• Building on the four skills of communication — listening, body language, speech, and expressive skills — two effective social skills resources are available specifically for teenagers: one is the Walker Social Skills ACCESS Curriculum available through ProEd at http://www.proedinc.com/customer/productView.aspx?ID=615 and the other is Skillstreaming, teaching prosocial skills to adolescents, available at http://www.researchpress.com/skillstreaming/adolescent/product/item/6576/. • Each of these resources are considered best practice for improving students' social and communication skills.	• Teachers, guidance counselors, and teen-oriented community organizations.

SELF-DETERMINATION AND
INTERPERSONAL SKILLS

Objectives	Activities/Strategies	Adult/Peer Roles
4. Demonstrate assertive communication when problem solving and resolving conflicts.	• Using the following suggested scenarios available through the National Crime Prevention Council for group discussion and problem solving: http://www.ncpc.org/ programs/teens-crime-and-the-community/community-works-session-enhancements/section-1/ session-7/role-play-scenarios.pdf. • Bully prevention activities can raise awareness of bullying, the types of bullying, and strategies to reduce or eliminate bullying in the school setting. The following website: http://library.thinkquest. org/TQ0312169/ is a site created by students for students who are 19 years and younger. This resource provides strategies and classroom materials.	• Teachers and peers in classroom or community settings utilizing the Five Steps to Conflict Resolution (Crawford and Bodine, 1996): 1. setting ground rules; 2. listening; 3. find a common interest; 4. brainstorm solutions; and, 5. discuss various points of view.

Domain: Self-Determination and Interpersonal Skills
Competency: 11. Being Self-Aware
Subcompetency: 46. Understand Personal Characteristics and Needs

Objectives	Activities/Strategies	Adult/Peer Roles
1. Understand physical characteristics.	• Students will draw a self-portrait indicating color, shape, and facial features unique to them. • Students will draw a portrait of a partner and vice versa, then they will compare what they think they look like to what someone else notices in them. • Discuss physical characteristics you think are special, unique, or favorites and why. • Describe physical differences between you and a friend. Discuss why you think those differences exist and who you received your different traits from (ex: I got my hair color from my grandmother).	

Objectives	Activities/Strategies	Adult/Peer Roles
2. Identify emotions.	• Watch clips from a movie and describe the characters' emotions or change in emotions as the story unfolds. • Ask parents how they felt when milestones or major events happened in the student's life. How did they celebrate or cope as a family? • Students will be given a picture of a person showing an emotion through facial expression. The student will write or narrate a story about why the person feels the way they do.	
3. Understand the effect of emotions and choices.	• Discuss events or read stories about events in history (slavery, war, natural disasters) and identify the event that caused an emotion. Discuss how the emotions felt may have triggered future events (federal aid, treaties, independence, grudges). • Students will identify how their emotions at home can cause events (being grounded, being respected, being praised or in trouble).	
4. Identify interests and abilities.	• If the school is able to fund this inventory, the student will take the Picture Interest Career Survey. • Students will take the O*Net survey online (PDF printable and free). • Students will identify an ability they have and teach a classmate/ family member how to do something that uses that specific ability (e.g., cooking, drawing, speaking in front of people, making YouTube videos, etc.).	
5. Identify character traits.	• Students will be given a story starter with a character that is faced with a hard decision. The student will complete the story ensuring the story character is using positive character traits in order to solve the problem (admitting a wrong doing, apologizing, returning something taken without permission, etc.). • Students will write personal goals to improve character traits they have identified as being a weakness. This will be shared with families so the student is kept accountable at home as well as school. • Students will participate in mock interviews where questions of their character are asked.	

SELF-DETERMINATION AND INTERPERSONAL SKILLS

Objectives	Activities/Strategies	Adult/Peer Roles
6. Identify current roles.	• Students will work with a partner and play the "Introduction Game" where they shake their partner's hand and say "Hi, I'm (name)," then "Hi, I'm a (daughter/son)," and continue by introducing themselves with as many labels/roles they can think of (sister, brother, reader, artist, employee, student, etc.). Then their partner takes a turn. • Students will create a draft resume and identify their roles under "work" or "volunteer experience" or "education" or "extracurricular activities."	
7. Identify possible future roles.	• Students will identify future jobs they would like to have, and, using a graphic organizer/web, students will write what that role entails, what skills are needed, what education is needed, who they know that is currently in that role (if any) and why they would choose that role. • Students will tour various workplaces within their community to learn about the roles available to them. Teachers should set up guided tours of stores/community centers.	
8. Understanding emotional and physical self-awareness as a component of self-determination.		

SELF-DETERMINATION AND
INTERPERSONAL SKILLS

Domain: Self-Determination and Interpersonal Skills
Competency: 11. Being Self-Aware
Subcompetency: 47. Identify needs: physical, emotional, social, and educational

Objectives	Activities/Strategies	Adult/Peer Roles
1. Identify physical needs.	• Students will keep a journal for a week and mark down each time they experience a physical need, how they feel, what they did, who they were with, etc. • Students will share their journal with their family. • Make a list of their physical needs, how many could be considered physical wants and why? • Go to the food pyramid website, http://www.mypyramid.gov/, for a quick estimate of what and how much students need to eat. Posters, interactive computer games, and education resources are also available at this site for review.	• Parents discuss and add to the journal. • Assist students with developing their own food pyramid for healthy eating.
2. Identify emotional needs.	• Students will keep a journal of their emotional needs: when do they feel happy, content, secure? Where was the student, who were they with, how did they react? • Students will volunteer at a charity and reflect on their experience of working with others and giving to someone in need. How did they feel and how did they help others?	• Parents discuss and add to the journal. • Assist students in locating and volunteering at a charity.
3. Identify social needs (communication, acceptance, respect, etc.).	• Survey peers about what clubs/sports they are involved in and why. • Join a club/sport at school. Reflect on your experience.	• Assist students with joining a club/sport at school.
4. Identify educational needs (study skills, organizational skills, executive functioning).	• Start using an agenda book to organize your homework and weekly class schedule. • Make a to-do list for each school day after reviewing your agenda book.	

Domain: Self-Determination and Interpersonal Skills
Competency: 11.Being Self-Aware
Subcompetency: 48. Identify Preferences: Physical Emotional, Social, and Educational

Objectives	Activities/Strategies	Adult/Peer Roles
1. Distinguish between needs and preferences.	• Students will understand the difference between needs and preferences. • Students will explore various objects to determine if the object is a need or a preference. • Students will apply concepts of needs and preferences to their own lives.	• Students will search their homes and list at least five needs and five preferences in their houses.
2. Identify physical preferences.	• Students will become aware of the variety of physical attributes. • Students will explore their own preferences in terms of physical attributes. • Students will apply personal physical preferences in their lives.	• With a peer, research online different exercise plans that you may be interested in participating in and share the activity with the class. • Research different hair styles and clothing styles that interest you and create a look book to refer to in the future. • For both activities you could incorporate www.pinterest.com to have the students make different boards for fitness and style.
3. Identify emotional preferences.	• Students will become aware of emotional preferences. • Students will explore various emotional preferences. • Students will apply emotional preferences to their own lives.	• Students write down the emotions of their family members and how they could tell what emotion they were feeling.
4. Identify social preferences.	• Students will be aware of various preferences in social situations. • Students will explore social preferences. • Students will apply their knowledge of social preferences to their own lives.	• Students will research online/ upcoming social activities in their community that they would be interested in participating in and list them on a calendar to refer to in the future.
5. Identify educational preferences.	• Students will become aware of various learning styles. • Students will explore various learning types. • Students will understand their unique educational preferences.	• Create a mini-lesson to teach to a peer in your preferred learning style and incorporate your preferred multiple intelligence domain.

Domain: Self Determination and Interpersonal Skills
Competency: 11. Being Self-Aware
Subcompetency: 49. Describe Others Perception of Self

Objectives	Activities/Strategies	Adult/Peer Roles
1. List potential reactions of others to one-self.	• Students will construct personal illustrated biographies of themselves in which they examine personality characteristics, personal goals and ambitions, and physical characteristics. • Students create a short computer-based presentation summarizing their biographies and seek feedback, public or private, to their presentation.	• Teacher and peer supports and guidelines must be established on communication and behavior of students toward one another for this deeply personal examination.
2. Construct a personal view of how others see one-self.	• Based upon feedback from activity above, students create a personal reflection on how they feel they are perceived by others. • Should students be concerned that their self-perception and the perceptions of others are not congruent, they can formulate a plan for changing what they are capable of changing.	
3. Describe the relationship between one's own behaviors and others' reactions.	• Students will observe their communication behavior (whether their statements were passive, aggressive, or assertive) and record others' reactions. This data recording activity should be conducted over at least 3 days with five to seven interactions per day. Students will record exactly what they said to another along with their perceived nonverbal communication, then the reaction of the other person. These should all be live conversations, not texts nor phone calls. Students will summarize their findings.	

SELF-DETERMINATION AND INTERPERSONAL SKILLS

Objectives	Activities/Strategies	Adult/Peer Roles
4. Demonstrate awareness of individual differences in others.	• The students discuss characters in short story literature and explain why they think the character thinks and/or behaves in the ways he or she does in the story. For a link to short story recommendations: http://www.midland-mi.org/gracedowlibrary/teen/pathfinders/ShortStories.pdf. • Students will enact certain scenes from the stories in class and state why they would or wouldn't react or behave in the same ways as the characters.	

Domain: Self-Determination and Interpersonal Skills
Competency: 11. Being Self-Aware
Subcompetency: 50. Demonstrate Awareness of How One's Behavior Affects Others

Objectives	Activities/Strategies	Adult/Peer Roles
1. List ways in which behavior affects others around us.	• For an entire day the students should smile and say hello to everyone they see and write down the response and how they felt about it.	• Teachers and peers
2. List appropriate behaviors for a variety of situations.	• Students will make a chart of appropriate behaviors for a variety of situations.	• Teachers and peers
3. List different cues elicited by others that behavior is inappropriate.	• Students will observe their surroundings, note when someone is acting inappropriately, and observe what other people do. • Students reflect on how their parents let them know they are acting inappropriately.	• Parents discuss the cues they give to their children.
4. List ways to correct inappropriate behavior.	• Students will reflect on a time they acted inappropriately. How could they have fixed that situation?	

Domain: Self-Determination and Interpersonal Skills
Competency: 12. Developing Interpersonal Skills
Subcompetency: 51. Demonstrating Listening and Responding Skills

Objectives	Activities/Strategies	Adult/Peer Roles
1. Identify proper listening and responding behaviors for casual and formal settings.	• The student will observe children and note when the child inappropriately speaks or listens to another's conversation. • Student will initiate a conversation at an appropriate time in the community (asking a question at a store, library, restaurant). • Student will practice different formalities of speaking with various people in the building (principal, secretary, teacher, friend, stranger, custodian, lunch aide).	
2. Identify positive outcomes of listening and responding appropriately.	• The student will write about a time they listened at an inappropriate time and what they heard that maybe they shouldn't have. • Play a short clip of a YouTube video or movie where there is strong dialogue. The student will give feedback and be able to answer questions about what they were talking about. • Student will give another student a multistep direction. Then they will switch roles.	
3. Identify negative aspects of listening and responding inappropriately.		

Domain: Self-Determination and Interpersonal Skills
Competency: 12. Developing Interpersonal Skills
Subcompetency: 52. Establish and Maintain Close Relationships

Objectives	Activities/Strategies	Adult/Peer Roles
1. Identify qualities of an individual who would be desirable as a dating partner.	• Students will discuss good qualities of a dating partner with an older sibling or parent.	• Parents/older siblings share their experiences with student.
2. Identify and demonstrate appropriate procedures for making a date.	• Students will practice with a friend how to accept a date. • Students will practice with a friend how to turn down a date.	• Friend plays the role of a person asking for a date.
3. List activities that are appropriate for a date.	• Students will discuss with a parent or older sibling some good places to go on a date. • Students will make a list of good dating ideas as students read magazines and watch TV.	• Parents/older siblings share their experiences with student.
4. Identify characteristics of close relationships.	• Students will discuss characteristics of close relationships with their parents.	• Parents share experiences and thoughts.
5. List different types of close relationships	• Students will make a list of different types of close relationships they have. • Students will make a list of different types of close relationships they see others have.	
6. Recognize and respond to the intimate feelings of others.	• Students will keep a journal of their feelings and others' feelings. • Students will share their journal with a parent or close friend.	• Parents share experiences.
7. Identify persons with whom one could establish a close relationship.	• Students will make a list of persons that they have a close relationship with. • Students will discuss with parents who they have close relationships with.	• Parents share experiences.

SELF-DETERMINATION AND INTERPERSONAL SKILLS

Domain: Self Determination and Interpersonal Skills
Competency: 12. Developing Interpersonal Skills
Subcompetency: 53. Make and Maintain Friendships

Objectives	Activities/Strategies	Adult/Peer Roles
1. Identify the necessary components of a friendship.	• Students will identify qualities of friends. • Students will distinguish between casual friends and close friends. • Students will explore friendship within the marriage relationship as representative of friendship in general. • Students will identify and illustrate the necessary components of a friendship.	• Students can work with their families to do a "Circle of Friends" map listing people that are very close to them, acquaintances, and people they work with daily.
2. List personal considerations in choosing a friend.	• Students will identify characteristics of someone they would like as a friend and someone they would not like as a friend. • Students will explore the process of making and keeping a friend.	• Teachers, peers, and parents can share experiences.
3. List rights and responsibilities important in personal friendships.	• Students will become aware of the rights and responsibilities involved in a friendship. • Students will be able to identify qualities one needs in relating to others. • Students evaluate rights and responsibilities in personal friendships.	• Discuss with students the risks of finding friends through social media. Also discuss safety online, using sites such as Facebook, Myspace, Twitter, etc.
4. List activities that can be shared with friends.	• Students will identify and explore activities that can be shared with friends. • Students will plan and conduct group activities to share with the class.	

Domain: Self-Determination and Interpersonal Skills
Competency: 12. Developing Interpersonal Skills
Subcompetency: 54. Develop and Demonstrate Appropriate Behavior

Objectives	Activities/Strategies	Adult/Peer Roles
1. Identify and demonstrate behavior appropriate to specific public settings.	• For an entire day, students will smile and say hello to everyone they see, then jot down how they responded and how they felt. • Take note of the behavior of someone students perceive to be well-respected and well-liked by others. How do they interact with others?	
2. Identify ways in which one's behavior affects others.	• Make a chart of appropriate behaviors for a variety of places, including school, work, home, and community settings. Record the extent to which students use these behaviors on a regular basis and what behaviors should they practice.	
3. Identify cues presented by others that one's behavior is inappropriate.	• Students will observe their surroundings, noting when someone is acting inappropriately and what what others around that person. How do they respond both verbally and nonverbally. • Reflect on how your peers, teachers, and parents let you know you are acting inappropriately.	• Peers, teachers, and parents discuss the cues they give to others for inappropriate behavior.
4. Identify ways to correct one's inappropriate behavior.	• Students will reflect on a time that they were inappropriate. Could they have fixed the situation? • Students will reflect on a time when a friend acted inappropriately. Did they suggest to them ways they could have behaved differently?	

SELF-DETERMINATION AND
INTERPERSONAL SKILLS

Domain: Self-Determination and Interpersonal Skills
Competency: 12. Developing Interpersonal Skills
Subcompetency: 55. Accept and Give Praise and Criticism

Objectives	Activities/Strategies	Adult/Peer Roles
1. Identify statements of praise in everyday activities.	• Students will keep a journal of praise statements that they hear throughout the day. • Give five compliments to friends and family.	• Parents discuss journals.
2. List appropriate and inappropriate responses to praise.	• Students will keep a journal of appropriate and inappropriate responses to the praise they give out to friends and family.	• Parents discuss journals.
3. Respond to praise statements by others.	• Students will ask a friend or parent to give them compliments so they can practice responding to praise.	
4. List the effects of praise on oneself.	• Students will keep a journal of how they feel when someone praises you.	
5. Identify critical and/or rejecting types of statements.	• Students will make make a list of critical or rejecting statements that they hear throughout the day.	
6. List appropriate ways to respond to criticism and/or rejection.	• Make a list of how they would respond to the list they made above.	
7. Respond appropriately to critical statements.	• Students will ask a friend or parent to give them critical statements, so they can practice responding.	
8. List positive and negative effects of criticism.	• Students will make a pros and cons chart of criticism.	• Teachers and peers role play strategies for ways to deal with critical comments in different situations including school, workplace, and other community settings. • Families and teachers describe ways in which positively-stated critical comments can be instructive and helpful.

Domain: Self-Determination and Interpersonal Skills
Competency: 13. Communicating With Others
Subcompetency: 56. Communicate With Understanding

Objectives	Activities/Strategies	Adult/Peer Roles
1. Identify and demonstrate methods of speaking appropriately in social conversations.	• Student will observe other cultures in the community (mall, restaurants) and identify communication characteristics. • Student will practice holding a conversation about a topic they are not familiar with by reading or listening and forming questions. • Student will identify communication characteristics that are socially accepted in their own families and compare it to classmates' findings.	

Domain: Self-Determination and Interpersonal Skills
Competency: 13. Communicating With Others
Subcompetency: 57. Know Subtleties of Communication

Objectives	Activities/Strategies	Adult/Peer Roles
1. Identify and demonstrate subtle or nonverbal elements of communication.	• Students will watch TV with the volume turned off. Determine what feelings the actors are portraying. • Students will review and reflect on this article about nonverbal communication http://www.helpguide.org/mental/eq6_nonverbal_communication.htm.	
2. Identify subtle verbal expressions that correspond to feelings.	• Students will keep a journal of their conversations with friends and family. Do their subtle expressions match their feelings? • Students will review this video on social cues http://www.youtube.com/watch?v=JYV2_AdiZJQ.	• Discuss journals with family or friends.
3. Identify verbal expressions that are inconsistent with feelings.	• Students will keep a journal of their conversations with friends and family. What feelings and expressions were inconsistent? Why?	
4. Demonstrate subtle verbal and nonverbal elements of communication.	• Students will practice subtle verbal and nonverbal elements of communication with their family.	• Parents and siblings interpret and demonstrate subtle verbal and nonverbal elements of communication.

Domain: Self Determination and Interpersonal Skills
Competency: 13. Communicating With Others
Subcompetency: 58. Assertive and Effective Communication

Objectives	Activities/Strategies	Adult/Peer Roles
1. Identify and demonstrate assertive communication behaviors.	• The student will understand the difference between four styles of communication. • The student will investigate aspects of assertive communication and distinguish between passive and assertive statements. • The student will understand how to apply techniques to become an assertive communicator.	• At home, students will observe their family members. They will determine which type of communicator each member is and write down an example that helped them come to that conclusion.
2. Demonstrate appropriate assertive communication behaviors.	• The students will demonstrate how assertive communication can be used in school. • The students will demonstrate how assertive communication can be used with family. • The students will demonstrate assertive communication in a variety of situations.	• Teachers utilize role play situations for practice. • Peer and self-evaluate communication behaviors.
3. Identify positive and negative outcomes associated with assertively communicating.	• The student will create a list of positive and negative outcomes of assertive communication and critically evaluate their list. • The student will create assertive statements and identify positive and negative outcomes of assertive communication. • The student will understand how assertive communication is used on the job.	• Practice being more assertive at home and record when and how you used assertive communication.

SELF-DETERMINATION AND INTERPERSONAL SKILLS

Domain: Self-Determination and Interpersonal Skills
Competency: 13. Communicating With Others
Subcompetency: 59. Recognize and Respond to Emergency Situations

Objectives	Activities/Strategies	Adult/Peer Roles
1. Identify sights and sounds of emergency situations.	• Students will identify and examine emergency situations in the home, at work, and in the community. • Students will describe the sights and sounds of emergency situations in the home, at work, and in the community. • Students will explore the sights and sounds of emergency situations while visiting a firehouse, emergency room, or police department. • Students will describe emergency situations, listing each emergency.	• Have students identify a time when they may have encountered an emergency and describe what they did or should have done.
2. Identify appropriate authorities to contact in emergency situations.	• Students will identify who to call during emergency situations. • Students will examine the occupation and services of different emergency authorities, including police, ambulance, and fire department personnel and volunteers. • Students will match emergency situations to the appropriate authority that needs to be called. • Students will develop a list of phone numbers for various emergency authorities and practice finding and spelling emergency authority words. • Students will demonstrate contacting the appropriate authorities in emergency situations.	• Research local emergency training or meetings for children. Arrange for the students to participate in one of these activities. • Call local fire stations to ask if students can visit the station to learn more about what will happen and who they will see if there was an emergency
3. Describe personal communication indicating emergency situations.	• Students will explore the different kinds of questions to ask a person in an emergency situation. • Students will identify nonverbal communication in emergencies. • Students will describe what one might say during an emergency situation.	• Students can interview somebody who works in emergency situations to discuss what they should do or say.
4. List personal responsibilities in emergency situations.	• Each student will identify different ways he or she could be of assistance in an emergency. • Students will understand different steps in the first-aid process. • Students will match the correct authority and phone number to given emergency situations. • Students will develop a list of items needed in a home medicine cabinet.	• Students will practice "applying" first aid care to family or friends at home.

SELF-DETERMINATION AND INTERPERSONAL SKILLS

Domain: Self-Determination and Interpersonal Skills
Competency: 14. Good Decision Making
Subcompetency: 60. Problem Solving

Objectives	Activities/Strategies	Adult/Peer Roles
1. Identify a problem and past experiences similar to this problem.	• Student will collaborate with other students on issues in the media they have read or heard about and identify the problem. They will answer who the problem is affecting and if it's negative or positive or both for others. • Student will interview family members and friends to compose a list of "problems." How are the problems different among different age groups?	
2. Identify desired outcome.	• Students will play a teacher-created version of "Would you rather" where the student has to decide between two choices that may potentially disadvantage another person. • Students will respond to made-up or real "Dear Abby" newspaper articles. They will help the letter writer solve a problem.	
3. Identify and describe options and possible outcome associated with options.	• The school social worker, psychologist and guidance counselor will visit the classroom to serve as a panel for students to ask questions about resources available. • Students will visit doctor's offices, libraries, or other community sites where brochures are provided for crisis hotlines or other social resources.	
4. Identify and access home and community resources and supports and choose best options.	• Draw "problem" cards that teacher has created prior to lesson. Students will lead a discussion on past experiences and the outcomes to similar problems.	
5. Demonstrate problem-solving behaviors.		

Domain: Self-Determination and Interpersonal Skills
Competency: 14. Good Decision Making
Subcompetency: 61. Identify and Set Goals

Objectives	Activities/Strategies	Adult/Peer Roles
1. Identify ways goal setting and attainment can affect one's life.	• Discuss with parents how they met their goals. How did it affect their lives?	
2. Identify potential goals.	• Using old magazines, make a collage of potential goals. Share your collage with parents.	
3. List possible outcomes to be considered when setting goals.	• Using list above, list possible outcomes to be considered. Discuss with parents.	
4. Determining a plan of action.	• Pick one of your goals and determine a plan of action. • Share your plan of action via a blog or social network. Reflect on feedback given by others and support.	

Domain: Self-Determination and Interpersonal Skills
Competency: 14. Good Decision Making
Subcompetency: 62. Develop Plans and Attain Goals

Objectives	Activities/Strategies	Adult/Peer Roles
1. Identify ways that goal attainment affects one's life.	• Each student will learn that planning how to achieve a goal is important and how achieving a goal can improve the student's life.	• Begin to think of a personal goal you would like to achieve either in school or at home.
2. List outcomes to be considered while attaining a goal.	• Each student will learn to create well defined goals to better help them achieve desired outcomes.	• Decide upon your goal.
3. Demonstrate goal attainment behavior.	• Each student will learn to prepare for obstacles to completing goals.	• Monitor your progress on achieving your goal with a parent or peer.

SELF-DETERMINATION AND INTERPERSONAL SKILLS

Domain: Self-Determination and Interpersonal Skills
Competency: 14. Good Decision Making
Subcompetency: 63. Self-Evaluation and Feedback

Objectives	Activities/Strategies	Adult/Peer Roles
1. Determine reasons why goal was or was not met.	• As a result of journaling activities (dialog journals may be appropriate for some students), students will create their own checklist of reasons for goals either being attained or not. • After reflecting on the checklist, students can decide what different actions or decisions (their own or those of others) either advanced or thwarted their goals.	
2. Determine positives and negatives of: problem solving, goal setting and attainment, and independent performance.	• Students can discuss either in small or whole groups the positive and negative outcomes of problem solving, goal setting, goal attainment, and independent performance. The positive and negative outcomes should be recorded as the students participate in the activity. A teacher or guidance counselor can facilitate the discussion and another adult record the students' statements.	

SELF-DETERMINATION AND
INTERPERSONAL SKILLS

Domain: Self-Determination and Interpersonal Skills
Competency: 14. Good Decision Making
Subcompetency: 64. Develop and Evaluate Alternatives

Objectives	Activities/Strategies	Adult/Peer Roles
1. Define the meaning of alternatives.	• Students will define the term "alternative" and give an example of an alternative. • Students will give examples of alternatives, considering time, budget, and ability factors. • Students will demonstrate an understanding of choosing alternatives to goals when considering the reasons for and benefits of those goals.	
2. List possible alternatives with respect to a personal goal.	• Students will identify alternatives to personal goals in several areas of life. • Each student will explore sources of help in identifying alternatives to personal goals. • Students will develop alternatives to personal goals in different areas of life.	• Students will talk to a family member or a peer to see if they ever had to make an alternative choice for one of their goals. Ask them how they felt about the alternative goal and why they chose that alternative.
3. Describe a compromise with respect to a personal goal.	• Students will define and explore the concept of compromise. • Students will explore the concept of compromise by asking a panel of married couples questions about compromising in a household. • Students will practice making compromises in personal goals.	• Talk to the student about a time when they had to compromise with someone. Discuss how it felt to compromise and how they came upon the compromise.
4. List resources for information that develops alternatives.	• Students will identify and explore the different resources for developing alternatives. • Students will develop a list of alternatives for career choices. • Students will develop a list of information resources for personal career choices.	

SELF-DETERMINATION AND INTERPERSONAL SKILLS

Domain: Self-Determination and Interpersonal Skills
Competency: 15.Developing Social Awareness
Subcompetency: 65. Develop Respect for the Rights and Properties of Others

Objectives	Activities/Strategies	Adult/Peer Roles
1. Identify personal and property rights of others.	• Students will compose a list of their rights and properties at home. They will also identify the rights and properties of the adults/other children in their household. • Provide students with a copy of procedural safeguards and their rights held under their IEP. Students can identify rights and responsibilities. • Discuss the privacy controls on Facebook and why it is smart to set privacy limits considering future bosses, people at school, family, etc.	
2. Identify a reason for respecting the rights and properties of others.	• Discuss the effects of posting pictures or comments about people on social network sites. • Interview an employee (could be a family member) and ask them what their rights are and how they know their rights. Review their employee handbook if possible. • Write about a make believe country and construct a list of rights the citizens will have (work in groups to complete).	
3. Demonstrate respect for others and their property.	• Watch the movie *Radio* and discuss what rights were disrespected and how it affected the other characters in the movie. • Hold a mock trial where students serve as jury members, defendants, and prosecutors where the case is on a personal property issue.	
4. List appropriate situations and procedures for borrowing the property of others.	• Students will make a list of items they would borrow and from whom. Explain why they wouldn't loan a certain item to just anybody (or a little brother or sister). • The student will ask a family member what they would feel comfortable loaning to to him or her and why they wouldn't loan certain things.	

SELF-DETERMINATION AND INTERPERSONAL SKILLS

Domain: Self-Determination and Interpersonal Skills
Competency: 15. Developing Social Awareness
Subcompetency: 66. Recognize Authority and Follow Instructions

Objectives	Activities/Strategies	Adult/Peer Roles
1. Identify common authority roles.	• Interview a person in an authoritative role. • In class, discuss different environments (school, workplace, community settings) and the individuals who would likely be in authoritative roles in each setting.	• Teacher or family help to locate a person to interview.
2. Identify aspects of following instructions.	• Play Simon Says with a friend or sibling.	• Provide internet access.
3. Identify situations in which the individual has the right to disregard instructions from authorities.	• Keep a journal of anytime you disregarded instructions from authorities and why. • Participate in a class discussion of situations in which students have disregarded rules and the outcomes. Describe more appropriate ways of following instructions.	• Discuss journal with parents.

Domain: Self-Determination and Interpersonal Skills
Competency: 15. Developing Social Awareness
Subcompetency: 67. Demonstrate Appropriate Behavior in Public Settings

Objectives	Activities/Strategies	Adult/Peer Roles
1. Identify appropriate behavior in public places.	• Students will become aware of inappropriate and appropriate behaviors in public. • Students will identify appropriate behaviors for public places. • The students will observe inappropriate behaviors and appropriate behaviors in an actual work setting. • Students will demonstrate appropriate public behavior.	• Throughout the week, students will write down any inappropriate behavior they observe during the day. Think of a behavior that would have been more appropriate in that situation.

Objectives	Activities/Strategies	Adult/Peer Roles
2. Identify and demonstrate appropriate behaviors when using transportation facilities.	• The students will identify appropriate behaviors when using transportation facilities. • Student will explore appropriate and inappropriate behaviors when using various means of transportation. • Each student will demonstrate appropriate public behavior when experiencing a transportation problem.	• If students ride the bus to school, have them observe how many others are engaging in inappropriate behavior. Tally them and note some of the inappropriate behaviors they are engaging in.
3. Identify and demonstrate appropriate behaviors when using eating facilities.	• Student will identify appropriate behaviors when using eating facilities. • Students will observe and record the eating behaviors of students in the school lunchroom. • Students will demonstrate the rules of etiquette to be used when eating in a public facility.	• Use the observation checklists from Lesson Plan 10 to rate the students when they go out to eat with their families.
4. Identify and demonstrate appropriate behaviors when using recreational facilities.	• The students will identify reasons for exhibiting appropriate behaviors in a recreational facility. • The students will identify recreational facilities and learn the rules for their use. • The students will identify behaviors that are appropriate when using a recreational facility. • The students will demonstrate appropriate behavior when using a recreational facility.	

Domain: Self-Determination and Interpersonal Skills
Competency: 15. Developing Social Awareness
Subcompetency: 68. Understand the Motivations of Others

Objectives	Activities/Strategies	Adult/Peer Roles
1. Identify and understand the motives of others in a given situation.	• Use the roll plays in the link below, and in addition to the questions provided, describe the motivations of the characters in each of the scenarios: http://www.ncpc.org/ programs/teens-crime-and-the-community/community-works-session-enhancements/section-1/ session-7/role-play-scenarios.pdf	
2. Identify the ways in which others' motives affect their decision-making.	• Students will make a chart of the characters in the role plays above or other role plays they use, and analyze each. Analyze each character's motivation and action or behavior. • Look at literature they are currently reading at home or at school. What are the character's motivations? Their behavior or actions? Do they get what they want? • Consider doing this type of analysis with some type of popular media or YouTube clip. Discuss the questions above as a whole group activity	
3. Incorporating the motives of others into one's decision-making.	• Have a class discussion on the typical ways that others' motivations affect the types of decisions we make (i.e., what our parents want for our future; what a significant other may want or not want in a relationship; what your coach or mentor may want that you may or may not want). • Have a class discussion on ways we can examine whether we are deciding something in our lives based upon the motivations of others or on our own motivation. Discuss effective assertive communication skills to help deal with situations in which the motivations of others are dictating unwanted or undesired actions or behavior.	

Domain: Self-Determination and Interpersonal Skills
Competency: 16. Understanding Disability Rights and Responsibilities
Subcompetency: 69. Identify and Understand Rights and Responsibilities

Objectives	Activities/Strategies	Adult/Peer Roles
1. Identify specific details (i.e., legislation, social movements, etc.) regarding the United States' disability rights movement (ADA, IDEA, Section 504, etc.).	• Reflect on how these specific cases have changed the outcome of students' lives — what impact did it have even if it was years before they were born?	
2. Identify your disability rights based on your disability across settings (elementary, secondary, and postsecondary education, employment, nationally etc.).	• Using http://www.tolerance.org/sites/default/files/documents/October_early_handout01.pdf as a guide, students examine the grounds of their school and use the guide and checklist to identify areas of need as far as equal access to materials and experiences among nondisabled and disabled students.	
3. Identify responsibilities to ensure your rights are not violated and what to do if they are violated.	• Students will examine all parts of their IEP to ensure they understand roles and responsibilities of those involved in their education program and transition goals, specially designed instruction, and related services. Be assertive in assuring your plan is being followed.	
4. Demonstrate self-awareness through demonstrating disability rights and responsibilities knowledge.	• Students will write a letter to their congressman about an issue they think needs to be addressed concerning the rights of those with disabilities.	

Domain: Self-Determination and Interpersonal Skills
Competency: 16. Understanding Disability Rights and Responsibilities
Subcompetency: 70. Identify and Appropriately Access Needed Services and Supports

Objectives	Activities/Strategies	Adult/Peer Roles
1. Identify needed services and supports to live successfully.	• Students will search the web for services and supports in their area. Be sure to contact local support agencies as well as the Social Security Administration, the Disability Rights Network in your state, advocacy organizations, and other supports services who can help students understand their rights as an adult.	• Families should support student's research and assist in application processes as needed. Parents can help prepare their student for agency interview questions, recording keeping, and decision making.
2. Determine how to appropriately access disability needed services and supports.	• Investigate service and support agencies online to identify contact information, services provided, costs, options for transportation, etc. If possible, students will visit local and state agencies with their family and determine which are appropriate for them while still in school and after graduation..	• Families should support student's research and assist in application processes as needed. Parents can help prepare their student for agency interview questions, recording keeping, and decision making.

EMPLOYMENT SKILLS

Domain: Employment Skills
Competency: 17. Knowing and Exploring Occupational Possibilities
Subcompetency: 71. Identify Personal Values Met Through Work

Objectives	Activities/Strategies	Adult/Peer Roles
1. List economic reasons for working at a job.	• Students list on chalkboard 15 activities they like to participate in, and what effort or cost is involved in each activity. • Students list on chalkboard 10 necessities of living and discuss whether the necessities are economically dependent upon someone working at a job. • Students list on chalkboard five activities and/or necessities that do not depend upon financial resources.	• Parents or peers discuss their first job and experiences with becoming economically independent.
2. Identify how a job affects building personal and social relationships.	• Students discuss being employed as a sense of belonging. • Students discuss the way in which a job allows one to form new friendships and social relationships. • Students discuss ways in which a work situation is similar to and different from other social situations. • Students list on chalkboard social activities in which coworkers engage outside the job.	• Parents or peers discuss their own experiences of making friends on the job. • Parents or peers discuss social activities they have shared with coworkers away from the job.
3. Identify personal needs that can be met through work.	• Students list on chalkboard the personal needs they feel work meets (e.g., fulfillment, satisfaction, self-esteem, self-respect, accomplishment, independence, security, socialization, etc.). • Students bring in pictures of workers who appear to be meeting their personal needs, and display them on poster board. • Students rank these needs met through work. • Students parallel school experiences with possible work experiences which meet personal needs.	• Parents discuss the concept of personal needs. • A working student explains how work meets his or her personal needs. • Guest speakers from the community discuss how their work helps them meet their personal needs.

EMPLOYMENT SKILLS

Objectives	Activities/Strategies	Adult/Peer Roles
4. Describe how work relates to one's self-esteem.	• Students define and discuss what self-esteem means to them. • Students bring in pictures of workers which appear to represent defined and discussed characteristics of self-esteem, and display them on poster board. • Students discuss the reasons why being employed allows one to value oneself. • Guidance counselor discusses the relationship of self-esteem to being gainfully employed. • Students interview workers in the community to gain their feelings about work.	• Parents define and discuss what self-esteem means to them. • A working student is invited to talk to the class and explain how work meets his or her self-esteem needs. • Guest speakers from the community discuss how their work helps them meet their self-esteem needs.

Domain: Employment Skills
Competency: 17. Knowing and Exploring Occupational Possibilities
Subcompetency: 72. Identify Societal Values Met Through Work

Objectives	Activities/Strategies	Adult/Peer Roles
1. Identify ways in which individual workers help society.	• Students identify workers who affect their daily lives. • Students exchange magazine pictures of workers and discuss their beliefs about how each worker in the picture contributes to society. • Teachers discuss their beliefs about how teaching contributes to society. • Students discuss the probable consequences of members of certain occupations not working. • Students list on chalkboard the roles of workers from different occupations. • Students discuss ways that workers contribute to society (e.g., purchasing goods and services, paying taxes).	• Parents or peers discuss their beliefs regarding the contribution of their jobs to society. • Parents or peers discuss how workers help maintain the standard of living in the community. • Members of unions, industries, or agencies present ways in which workers are important to the community.
2. Identify ways in which members of a specific occupation contribute to society.	• Students list on chalkboard specific services provided by major occupations. • Class takes field trips to observe members of different occupations at work. • Students are assigned a specific occupation to investigate. • Students create a display on the bulletin board which lists specific occupations and their major contributions. • Students role-play members of different occupations and discuss the importance of their jobs.	• Parents or peers discuss their jobs and contributions to the community. • Member of the Chamber of Commerce identifies major local industries and jobs, and discusses contributions to the community. • Representatives from local industries identify contributions to the community. • Representative from nonprofits and community agencies identify services, supports, and available community initiatives and opportunities for participation.

Objectives	Activities/Strategies	Adult/Peer Roles
3. Identify ways in which workers on different jobs are interdependent.	• A qualified person in the community gives a presentation covering major occupations involved in meeting our daily needs. • Students discuss what would be different if one of the major occupations mentioned did not exist, and what other occupations would be affected as a result of the absence. • Students identify relationships between jobs in different communities.	• Parents or peers discuss the interdependence of their jobs. • Government official discusses the interdependence of business, industry, farming, and government. • Workers from a specific occupation discuss their dependence on members of other occupations.
4. Describe ways society rewards different occupations.	• Students discuss fringe benefits which society considers rewards based on the job (e.g., sick leave, vacation time, working conditions, etc.). • Students discuss the benefits which are considered rewards by society. • Given a list of occupations available locally, students identify occupations that provide high income. • Given the same list of occupations, students identify occupations that provide high esteem. • Given the same list, students identify occupations that provide both high income and high esteem.	• Parents or peers identify the aspects of their jobs for which society rewards them. • Guest speakers from various occupations discuss societal rewards.

Domain: Employment Skills
Competency: 17. Knowing and Exploring Occupational Possibilities
Subcompetency: 73. Identify Remunerative Aspects of Work

Objectives	Activities/Strategies	Adult/Peer Roles
1. Identify why people are paid for working.	• Students look at pictures of people performing different jobs. • Students are given a worksheet to complete, telling the reasons for going to school and the type of job and income they hope to obtain from attending school. • Students list on chalkboard the kinds of goods and services different jobs provide for the community. • Students discuss community needs for certain goods and services. • Students discuss their own experiences with paid employment. • Students choose two jobs and verbally explain the reasons why a person would be paid for performing each job (e.g., services performed, time spent on job, education and/ or training required to perform the job, etc.). • Students discuss other forms of remuneration.	• Parents or peers discuss what their jobs are and why they are getting paid. • Workers from different jobs discuss their job responsibilities and types of remuneration.
2. Identify why some jobs pay better than others.	• Students look at pictures of people performing jobs and explain the differences between jobs regarding education, training, and time spent on the job. • Students identify general categories of jobs along with training, education, and rate of pay. • Students research jobs that they are interested in, identifying the level of training and education needed. • Students take field trips to job sites to discuss requirements for employment at those sites. • Students discuss the salary they expect to be paid, based on their training and experience. • Students discuss why some jobs pay by the hour while others are salaried.	• Parents discuss requirements for their jobs and the rate of pay. • Workers or peers discuss the relationship of requirements and demands for their jobs to salary.

EMPLOYMENT SKILLS

Objectives	Activities/Strategies	Adult/Peer Roles
3. Discuss personal needs that are met through wages.	• Students discuss 10 personal needs. • Students discuss what needs they hope to meet with their salaries. • Students list on chalkboard necessary payments which must be deducted from one's salary (e.g., rent , food, etc.). • Students discuss fringe benefits of a work situation (e.g., retirement, education, planning for the future, medical, security, etc.) and how these satisfy personal needs.	• Peers or parents discuss budgeting their income. • Peers or parents discuss needs that are directly or indirectly met by wages (e.g., necessities, luxuries, recreation, etc.). • Parents discuss their own wages with students.
4. Discuss positive and negative aspects of different kinds of wages.	• Students discuss differences of wage earnings. • Students compute salaries based on various rates of pay. • Students discuss purchasing ability based upon wages calculated.	• Recent graduates receiving various kinds of wages discuss positive and negative aspect of their experiences. • Persnnel officer explains different wages paid in his or her setting.
5. Given a paycheck stub, calculate deduction information.	• Teacher provides students with several paycheck stubs and reviews on chalkboard deduction information. • Students calculate balance of initial income given, from a list of prescribed taxable deductions.	

SAMPLE LESSON PLAN 13   **17.73..5A:13**

LCE Objective 17.73.5: Given a paycheck stub, calculate deduction information.

Lesson Objective: Student will define types of deductions.

Instructional Resources: Worksheet Important Vocabulary.

Lesson Introduction: A number of terms appear on a paycheck stub. You need to be familiar with the meaning of each term.

School Activity: **Time:** 1 session

Task:

1. Discuss the concept of deductions, for example, large yearly payments for insurance or taxes divided into smaller amounts that are subtracted from each monthly check by your employer. Explain that the amount of money a person earns is not the same as the amount available to spend. Total earnings are referred to as gross pay; net pay represents the amount left after certain deductions.

2. Describe each of the following deductions:

    *   FICA – deduction for Social Security benefits paid at retirement or illness.
    *   Federal income tax – payment withheld for federal income taxes.
    *   State tax – payment withheld for state income taxes.
    *   City tax – payment withheld for city income tax.
    *   Pension – deduction for a retirement program.
    *   401K – individual retirement savings plan.
    *   Union dues – deduction for monthly dues to union or professional organization.
    *   Voluntary savings – savings deductions, e.g., U.S. savings bonds.
    *   Health, life, and/or disability insurance – deductions for insurance payments.

3. Students complete Worksheet Important Vocabulary in pairs and review definitions in class.

Lesson Plan Evaluation:

Activity: Students will complete the worksheet.

Criteria: Student will correctly define 8 out of 10 terms.

EMPLOYMENT SKILLS

Domain: Employment Skills
Competency: 17. Knowing and Exploring Occupational Possibilities
Subcompetency: 74. Locate Sources of Employment and Training Information

Objectives	Activities/Strategies	Adult/Peer Roles
1. List sources of employment information.	• Take a look at the Occupational Outlook website: www.bls.gov/oco • Review Career Track's website: http://careertrack.org. • Students will take the career test to see what career fits their personality at: http://www.careertest.net. • Check out: http://www.monster.com.	• Teachers, parents, or peers assist in identifying and categorizing several selected occupations.
2. List information provided by the sources from objective 1.	• After reviewing the above websites, create a spreadsheet of jobs, starting pay, benefits, location, ways in which job is a good fit, etc.	• Teachers and parents provide guidance in understanding implications of job search.
3. Use employment information sources to demonstrate how to obtain information specific to a job.	• Review the website for training information.	
4. Locate sources of training information.		• Teachers, employment counselors, and rehabilitation counselors discuss job classifications and training required for types of jobs. • Parents discuss classifications of jobs, e.g., skilled, unskilled, professional, technical, etc. • A career counselor presents program identifying sources of occupational information available (e.g., State Employment Offices, Department of Labor Office, The Division of Vocational Rehabilitation Offices, Dictionary of Occupational Titles, Occupational Outlook Handbook) • Visit your local unemployment office for training information. • Visit local community college for specific educational and training opportunities.

EMPLOYMENT SKILLS

Domain: Employment Skills
Competency: 17. Knowing and Exploring Employment Possibilities
Subcompetency: 75. Classify Jobs Into Employment Categories

COMPETENCY UNITS   123

Objectives	Activities/Strategies	Adult/Peer Roles
1. Locate jobs using Yellow Pages and want ads.	• Students will go to http://www.yellowpages.com/ and search through local businesses that may interest them. Carefully read ways in which the applicant is to contact human resources. Often stopping by or even a phone call is not appropriate; many employers look for online application submissions. • Use familiar search engine to find students' local newspaper and search the want ads section.	• Provide internet access and guidance in choosing businesses. • Provide support to access applications.
2. Locate occupational categories and sort jobs into different occupational categories.	• Using the Yellow Pages website above, list the jobs students found in the following categories: skilled, unskilled, indoor, outdoor. • Go to http://www.bls.gov/soc/ and locate students' chosen jobs' occupational categories.	• Provide guidance in choosing categories.
3. Locate information about job classifications.	• Go to http://www.job-hunt.org/ and locate your state employment office's website. Look up information about job classifications.	• Provide internet access. • Take students to the state employment office. • Employment counselor or work experience coordinator discusses job opportunities available locally in various job classifications.
4. List major categories of jobs related to interest.	• Take the interest inventory survey at http://www.edonline.com/newtest2/index.html. • Use information provided from the survey to list major categories of jobs related to the provided interests.	• Provide internet access and support in categorization of jobs, need for training, salaries, opportunities for promotion, etc.
5. List general job categories.	• Review the general job clusters at the bottom of this website: http://www.doe.in.gov/achievement/career-education/indiana-college-career-pathways.	• Parents, teachers, or peers discuss classification of jobs (e.g., skilled, unskilled, professional, technical, etc.).
6. Locate training requirements and wages for common job classifications.	• Contact friends and family members who have jobs you are interested in. Ask them about training and wages. • Go to http://www.careeronestop.org/ and look into training opportunities in your chosen job category. • Check with Community College representatives regarding education and training in various employment categories.	• Teachers, families and peers support.

EMPLOYMENT SKILLS

Domain: Employment Skills
Competency: 17. Knowing and Exploring Occupational Possibilities
Subcompetency: 76. Investigate Local Occupational and Training Opportunities

Objectives	Activities/Strategies	Adult/Peer Roles
1. Select an occupational area and find local employers in the Yellow Pages.	• Use search engines on Monster.com, Careerbuilder.com, Dice.com, and craigslist.org to locate possible job opportunities. • Visit yellowpages.com to locate possible employers. • Use online maps to find the location of employers and the distance from home to the possible employer. • Narrow search to specific cities, jobs, skills and training needed. • Post resume online for various sites listed above.	• Student, family, and peers provide support in creating a spreadsheet and keeping records of pertinent occupational information.
2. Collect and read help wanted ads in the occupational areas selected in objective 1.	• Print job descriptions obtained from websites listed in Objective 1 and highlight concerns/questions to ask another adult. • Print job descriptions obtained from websites listed in Objective 1 and list skills students have that match the job. • Print job descriptions obtained from websites listed in Objective 1 and list skills students do *not* have that match the job. • Identify categories within the job descriptions found on the websites listed in Objective 1 to determine if the job is a good match (categories: skills needed, education, hours, pay, location).	• Student discusses with family members jobs they have had, characteristics of the work, what they enjoy, what they didn't like about that job, and whether they can offer any advice.
3. Utilize sources of employment information.	• Visit job fairs held at community centers, schools, etc. • If a "Transition Fair" is available, visit booths to gather information/pamphlets on services for employment. • Check the newspaper for Help Wanted ads on a daily/weekly basis • Participate in career skills day, if available, to help build interviewing skills and employment information.	• Member of the local Chamber of Commerce discusses employment opportunities in the community.

EMPLOYMENT SKILLS

Objectives	Activities/Strategies	Adult/Peer Roles
4. Locate sources of employment information.	• Check the newspaper on a daily basis to find employment information (as mentioned in objective 3). • Visit state employment websites to locate information on jobs and postings. • Visit grocery stores for Help Wanted ads. • Search for jobs online. Include in the search the city and state.	• Student and family record pertinent employment information from resources.

Domain: Employment Skills
Competency: 18. Knowing and Exploring Employment Possibilities
Subcompetency: 77. Identify Major Employment Interests

Objectives	Activities/Strategies	Adult/Peer Roles
1. Identify occupational categories of interest.	• Using the information from the online career interest survey (http://www.edonline.com), match interests to job categories. This website also takes in to account the student's learning style. • Collect various job ads (online, grocery stores, newspaper, etc.) and categorize them by service industry, fast food, community worker, business, etc. • With the collected job ads mentioned above, list the education and skills required to determine if it is a good match for you.	• Teachers, families, and peers discuss why they find certain jobs more appealing and realistic than others.
2. Rank areas of personal interest in order of importance in finding an occupation.	• Have guest speakers visit the classroom from various careers to discuss their struggles with scheduling, pay, workload, hours, etc. to give students an idea of what employment is like. • Have a discussion circle (could include the guest speakers) about what is important in a job. • Students will make a list of their "perfect job" including hours, training, labor involved, skills involved. • Given several job ads, the student will rank them by most favorable to least favorable and be able to explain why they ranked them the way they did.	

Objectives	Activities/Strategies	Adult/Peer Roles
3. Identify how interests relate to jobs.	• Visit a place of employment and job shadow someone performing a job that is of low interest and reflect on how the day went — pros/cons of the job position. • On a two-column chart, the student's interests in one column and a job that matches the interests in the other column (ex: I love animals: dog walker).	• Teachers, families, and peers discuss demands of jobs, how jobs might relate to student interests, etc.
4. Describe ways the chosen job of interest relates to future personal goals.	• Refer back to the personal goals set in 14.61 and create a thinking map that describes how the job of interest connects to future goals. • On the two-column chart mentioned in Objective 3, add a third column where the student will describe the connection between interest and job. • Practice interviewing skills based on this objective: Ask the student, "Why do you want this job?" and and have them verbally explain how their interests lead up to their own personal goals in life.	• Student teacher/peers work on group activities in the classroom and with families at home.

Domain: Employment Skills
Competency: 18. Exploring Employment Choices
Subcompetency: 78. Identfiy Employment Aptitudes

Objectives	Activities/Strategies	Adult/Peer Roles
1. Identify different aptitudes necessary in the performance of various jobs	• Using the job ads from 18.77, list the different aptitudes needed and rank them 1-5, 5 being "expert" or "very skilled" and 1 being "novice" or "beginner." • Job shadow someone in the field of interest and take notes on skills needed to perform that job and the level of aptitude.	• Parents explain to students how aptitudes (abilities) relate to job performance.
2. Identify personal aptitudes.	• Visit careerexplorer.net to identify personal aptitudes. • Review the following website for videos of various jobs: http://www.careeronestop.org/ Audience/Professionals/CCA/ CareerExplorationandVideos.aspx.. • Rank personal aptitudes to help narrow a job search. Have the student, teacher, and parent rank and review the data together to discuss any discrepancies.	• Student/Family/Teacher support in class and home activities.

EMPLOYMENT SKILLS

Objectives	Activities/Strategies	Adult/Peer Roles
3. Identify activities that could improve personal aptitude necessary for a preferred job.	• From the inventory in the 2nd objective (student/teacher/parent responses), discuss options for growth in low areas (ex: summer school, volunteer opportunities for experience, remedial tutoring, social skills). • Interview someone in the field of choice and discuss activities that may be beneficial for that specific field that would build on the skills needed to perform duties. • Check community center schedules for classes or clubs that will improve skills needed. • Student creates a list of activities he or she would like to do and link them to skills needed for specific careers. • Check community center schedules for workshops or camps that may help improve skills needed.	

Domain: Employment Skills
Competency: 18. Knowing and Exploring Employment Possibilities
Subcompetency: 79. Investigate Realistic Employment Choices

Objectives	Activities/Strategies	Adult/Peer Roles
1. Identify major employment interest.	• Interview people in the community on why they chose their career. • Students may want to try CareerShip at: http://mappingyourfuture.org	• Teachers/peers/family discuss which aspects of different jobs are most and least important to them.
2. Identify employment aptitudes.	• Student will complete the Reality Check Worksheet at: http://schools.utah.gov/cte/cteintro_cda.html • "Reality Check" worksheet	• Family assist student with the "reality check" worksheet to discuss appropriate employment options based on realistic aptitudes, preferences, and availability.
3. Investigate realistic employment choices.	• Students investigate the following websites in helping determine desired, realistic career choices: - http://schools.utah.gov/cte/cteintro_cda.html - http://mappingyourfuture.org/planyourcareer/careership/ - http://www.careergames.com	• Student/family visit job sites that reflect their interests.

EMPLOYMENT SKILLS

Objectives	Activities/Strategies	Adult/Peer Roles

4. Identify requirements of desired and available employment.	• Students investigate the following websites in helping determine desired, realistic career choices:
	  - http://www.powertolearn.com/ teachers/lesson_activities/careers/ CBV.127.E.CAR.R4.F_912.pdf
	  - http://www.careergames.com/
	  - http://www.gcic.peachnet.edu/ RD/brochure/Middle/6gls/ School6G.htm
		• Student/family along with teachers and peers investigate, conduct mock interviews, and seek out job-shadowing experiences.

5. Identify major employment needs.	• Students investigate the following websites in helping determine desired, realistic career choices:
	  - http://www.powertolearn.com/ teachers/lesson_activities/careers/ CBV.124.S.CAR.R4.D1_58.pdf
	  - http://www.careergames.com/
		• Student/family discuss postschool working and living arrangements, number of hours.

Domain: Employment Skills
Competency: 18. Knowing and Exploring Employment Possibilities
Subcompetency: 80. Identify Requirements of Desired and Available Employment

Objectives	Activity	Adult/Peer Roles
1. Identify the availability and location of jobs.	• Student will use www.monster.com and www.snagajob.com to locate identify openings and narrow the locations of desired jobs. • Student will check statistics on job availability at www.bls.gov/ audience/students. • Check the statistics on job availability.	• Parents help the student obtain information about specific requirements for each job. • Parents discuss with the student desirable and undesirable jobs.
2. List specific job-related requirements.	• Using www.monster.com and www. snagajob.com, students willview the criteria for the job position. • Students will identify (. . .) requirements are at www.bls.gov/ k12/index.htm (Bureau of Labor Statistics). Identify desired positions on the government's website and see what the requirements are, http:// www.bls.gov/k12/index.htm (Bureau of Labor Statistics).	• Parents help the student obtain information about the demands of each of these jobs.

Objectives	Activity	Adult/Peer Roles
3. Identify an alternative for each occupation for which personal qualifications are not commensurate with identified requirements.	• Visit websites such as http://www.careerbuilder.com/Article/CB-1252-Who-is-Hiring-20-Jobs-You-Can-Get-With-a-High-School-Diploma/ to identify jobs that only require a high school diploma. • Identify a desired position and consider the job one might have before receiving that position (career ladder).	• Parents help the student identify the kinds of demands he or she may be unable to meet. • Parents help the student identify alternative, desirable, and realistic employment available in the community.

Domain: Employment Skills
Competency: 18. Knowing and Exploring Employment Possibilities
Subcompetency: 81. Identify Major Employment Needs

Objectives	Activity	Adult/Peer Roles
1. Identify needs that can be met through one's occupation and rank them in order of personal preference.	• Look through an employer's handbook to find the benefits of the position desired. Rank them as to how they meet students' individual needs. • Students will interview someone in their desired field and list the benefits mentioned that meet their needs (go in with a checklist of needs to be met).	• Parents discuss with students needs which are met my their jobs and rank their needs in order of importance to family and personal preference.
2. Identify personal-social needs met through work.	• Job shadow for a day and list the social needs that were met during that time.	• Employees from different occupational environments discuss or demonstrate what it is like to work in their respective environments.
3. Name status needs met through work.	• Job shadow for a day and list the status needs that were met during that time. • Students will interview someone in their desired field and list the positive attributes of the status the position gives	• Parents, teachers, or peers discuss and define status needs met through work.

EMPLOYMENT SKILLS

Objectives	Activity	Adult/Peer Roles
4. Identify factors that the student needs in a personal occupational environment.	• Students construct on poster board a hierarchy of major personality characteristics (e.g., likes, dislikes, need for structure, etc.) one would attempt to meet in selecting an occupation. • Group discussion on counseling allows the student to identify his or her own personality characteristics as well as sensory environmental aspects of different types of employment and workplace settings. • Vocational counselor discusses the responsibilities involved in various occupations	
5. Identify the most personally satisfying aspects and the least satisfying aspects about a specific job.	• Research a job on the internet (www.monster.com, www.snagajob.com, www.careerbuilder.com) and identify things the student would like or dislike about it. • Job shadow and create a reflective list of things the student enjoyed/did not enjoy	• Teacher/peers and the family assist in helping determine the most and least satisfying aspects of a particular job or workplace environment.
6. Identify criteria one would use in selecting an occupation.	• Create a list of needs (financial/social/location/status) to compare a job to.	• Student and family create a spreadsheet with indicators to help student make comparisons and assist in employment decisions.

Domain: Employment Skills
Competency: 19. Seeking, Securing, and Maintaining Employment
Subcompetency: 82. Search for a Job

EMPLOYMENT SKILLS

Objectives	Activities/Strategies	Adult/Peer Roles
1. Identify the steps involved in searching for a job.	• Review the steps involved in the job search tutorial at http://www.job-hunt.org/starting.shtml. • Contact your guidance counselor, friends, neighbors, etc. about job openings in your area. • Go to your local mall, grocery stores, convenience store, and/or post office and look for posted help wanted ads.	• Representative from the State Employment Service discusses preliminary job search procedures. • Provide transportation or community-based instruction opportunities • Class role-plays step-by-step procedures in job search.

Objectives	Activities/Strategies	Adult/Peer Roles
2. Identify a potential job through employment resources.	• Search websites like http://www.monster.com, http://www.job-hunt.org/, and Craigslist for potential jobs in your area.	• Families work with students to investigate online and print employment resources. • As it applies to the student, a vocational rehabilitation counselor presents discussion of services through that agency.
3. Arrange a real or simulated job interview.	• Review interview advice at http://career-advice.monster.com/job-interview/careers.aspx. • Watch video at http://www.youtube.com/watch?v=KFeGt_vHd1k&feature=related. • Ask a friend or family member to practice interview questions.	• Teachers, families, and peers to help with interview preparation • Set up a mock interview.

Domain: Employment Skills
Competency: 19. Seeking, Securing, & Maintaining Employment
Subcompetency: 83. Apply for a Job

Objectives	Activities/Strategies	Adult/Peer Roles
1. Identify appropriate job application procedures.	• Discuss job application procedures with classmates, family, and friends, ask them for tips. • Identify unique guidelines for application submissions (online, in person, mail, etc.). • Identify unique guidelines for references (written letters, phone contacts, etc).	• Class reviews job application forms from various businesses. • Students construct a display on a bulletin board depicting the do's and don'ts of applying for a job.
2. Collect a personal data sheet to be used for job application.	• Create a one page personal data sheet to carry with you when applying for jobs. • Make extra copies.	• Class takes a field trip to a local community college to discuss their personal data sheets with job placement counselor, vocational resource educator, or other counselors providing that service.

EMPLOYMENT SKILLS

Objectives	Activities/Strategies	Adult/Peer Roles
3. Complete a real or simulated job application with spelling assistance.	• Complete a practice job application at http://www.quintcareers.com/ employment_application.pdf. • Print out a blank application to practice hand writing neatly or online submissions which must be word processed for submission.	• Families and teachers provide internet access.
4. Apply for a real or simulated job in person or by telephone.	• Practice applying for a job at home with your parents • Utilize job shadowing, work experiences, volunteer opportunities, or internships to spend time in the workplace. • Call a local business to apply for a job. • Travel to local businesses, agencies, or organizations likely to hire and apply for a job.	• Families or teachers provide support and transportation.

Domain: Employment Skills
Competency: 19. Seeking, Securing, and Maintaining Employment
Subcompetency: 84. Interview for a Job

Objectives	Activities/Strategies	Adult/Peer Roles
1. Obtain an interview or carry out a mock interview.	• Go to the following website and practice your responses to the mock interview questions. • Utilize YouTube resources on interview tips: http://www.youtube.com/watch?v=epcc9X1aS7o http://www.youtube.com/watch?v=0p_A2P_uvzc • Practice a mock interview with family members. • Students construct a display on a bulletin board illustrating the various stages of an interview and the types of behavior required. • Guidance counselor presents a discussion of proper interview behavior.	• Parents help to role-play an interview. • Students role-play and videotape job interviews, then peer- and self-assess their performances.
2. Identify interview behaviors.	• Go to the following website and review "avoiding bad interview behaviors": http://career-advice.monster.com/job-interview/interview-preparation/how-bizarre-avoiding-bad-interview-behavior-hot-jobs/article.aspx.	• Teachers and family provide internet access.
3. Complete a real or simulated job interview.	• Apply for a job and go to your first interview. • Use questions above to hold a simulated interview with friends or family members.	• Parents discuss different ways to obtain a job interview. • Parents discuss what is involved in each method. • Parents or peers role-play obtaining an interview. • A job placement specialist gives a presentation on the do's and don'ts of obtaining a job interview. • Parents role-play or practice interviews with the student. • Personnel officers or interviewers discuss good and bad interview behaviors. • Parents discuss with the student how to behave in a job interview. • Parents or peers role-play a job interview with the student. • Parents or peers help the student correct any inappropriate behavior he or she displays in the role-play. • Employers discuss their expectations for interviews. • Former students, peers, and young adults discuss their experiences with the entire procedure from job search to employment.

EMPLOYMENT SKILLS

Objectives	Activities/Strategies	Adult/Peer Roles
4. Obtain transportation to and from the interview.	• Students discuss means of transportation available to them. • Students identify an interview site and list on chalkboard the means of getting there. • Students practice identifying different locations and discussing which means of transportation to use in getting to each. • Students discuss the importance of punctuality to the interview.	• Parents help the student identify all available means of transportation. • Employment personnel discusses punctuality for the interview and on the job.

Domain: Employment Skills
Competency: 19. Seeking, Securing, and Maintaining Employment
Subcompetency: 85. Solve Job-Related Problems

Objectives	Activities/Strategies	Adult/Peer Roles
1. Identify potential problems encountered on the job.	• Students discuss how one might deal with these problems. • Students role-play problem situations.	• Make a list of potential problems encountered at the workplace. • From that list, discuss with a friend and/or family member how to avoid such problems. • An employer gives a presentation on the kinds of problems one typically encounters on a job. • Teachers and families share any experiences in the workplace in which a problem was resolved; note any common patterns in the problem-solving process. • School counselor talks about the kinds of problems typically encountered in adjusting to any new situation (e.g., making friends, adjusting to new routines, etc.).
2. For potential problems, identify possible solutions.	• Go to the following website for tips on how to resolve workplace problems: http://spot.pcc.edu/~rjacobs/career/resolving_workplace_problems.htm. • Discuss the above suggestions with a friend and/or family member. • Students role-play problem. resolution, with each student playing the role of the supervisor. • Students discuss what might be done at work to minimize these problems.	• Provide internet access. • Families, teachers, and peers conduct role-play scenarios and follow-up discussion.

Objectives	Activities/Strategies	Adult/Peer Roles
3. Identify resources for assistance if problems cannot be personally resolved.	• Review the following website for agencies who can assist you with problems at work: http://www.direct.gov.uk/en/Employment/ResolvingWorkplaceDisputes/DG_199634. • The following US government site has many resources for employment for people with disabilities: http://www.dol.gov/odep/.	• Provide internet access. • Families, teachers, and peers review and evaluate resources for employment issues that are not resolved by typical collaboration and problem solving.

Domain: Employment Skills
Competency: 19. Seeking, Securing, and Maintaining Employment
Subcompetency: 86. Functions of Meeting and Exceeding Job Standards

Objectives	Activities/Strategies	Adult/Peer Roles
1. Determine the competitive level of skill and performance required for essential functions of a specific job.	• Narrow the student's job selection down to a specific job. • Ask to job shadow this specific job. • Make a list of skills needed for this specific job. • Determine the competitive level and how students will meet it. • Students prepare a chart of the specific job requirements and their own aptitude and abilities.	• Provide or assist with transportation to job shadowing. •
2. Identify potential remedial activities that might be required by an occupation.	• Make a list of what skills students need to improve. • Plan how students will achieve these skills. • Utilize online resources available through the Department of Labor website, for example, Skills that Pay the Bills, http://www.dol.gov/odep/topics/youth/softskills/softskills.pdf	• Teachers and families provide support and guidance. • Guidance counselors consult on course of study. • Visit local community college and discuss plan with job placement counselor on achieving job skills.
3. Determine the level of personal abilities required for a specific occupation.	• Reevaluate job skills to determine fit of personal aptitudes and abilities with specific occupation. • Make decisions about whether specific job is realistic, given aptitude and abilities.	• Provide support and guidance.

EMPLOYMENT SKILLS

Domain: Employment Skills
Competency: 19. Seeking, Securing, and Maintaining Employment
Subcompetency: 87. Maintain and Advance in Employment

Objectives	Activities/Strategies	Adult/Peer Roles
1. Identify factors that determine successful maintenance of employment.	• Make a list of factors that determine successful employment • Go to the following website and review how to be a good employee http://www.wikihow.com/Be-a-Good-Employee.	• Teachers and families provide internet access.
2. Identify factors that determine unsuccessful maintenance of employment.	• From the website above, make a list of things to avoid at work.	• Teachers, families and peers review "don'ts" with student and describe outcomes of continuing inappropriate habits and behaviors at work.
3. Identify potential employment variations within a specific occupation.	• From students' previous job-shadowing experience, discuss the job variations available.	• Teachers and peers share job shadowing of similar job in various settings, discuss positive factors and negative factors of each.
4. Identify factors that lead to termination of employment.	• Make a list of factors that may get someone fired from a job. • Make a plan of how to avoid such factors.	• Parents relate experiences with fellow workers who have been fired or forced to resign. • Parents or peers discuss significant differences between employees possessing jobs with the same title. • Parents help the student identify major responsibilities of several potential jobs. • Representatives of several occupations discuss responsibilities that exist in all jobs. • Representatives from various companies discuss their employee expectations and their process of termination.
5. Identify factors that lead to advancement in employment.	• Go to the following website and review ways to advance a career: http://www.careerbuilder.com/Article/CB-898-Getting-Ahead-9-Little-Known-Ways-to-Advance-Your-Career/	• Parent or peers discuss with students the factors or reasons for their promotions. • Company representative presents to class factors leading to employment promotions.

EMPLOYMENT SKILLS

Domain: Employment Skills
Competency: 20. Exhibiting Appropriate Employment Skills
Subcompetency: 88. Follow Directions and Observe Regulations

Objectives	Activities/Strategies	Adult/Peer Roles
1. Perform a series of tasks in response to verbal instructions.	• Provide students with something to build or put together (hamburger, model, folder of papers, roll of silverware, etc) and have them use verbal directions to complete the activity. • Have students view a YouTube video that gives verbal directions on how to complete a task, such as How to Tie a Tie: http://www.youtube.com/watch?v=MbXzI-IAdSc • Have students reflect on what was easy/difficult with that task.	• Student/teacher/family work on specific activities in which single and multiple instructions must be followed for task completion. Experiment with various cuing systems when multiple or serial instructions involved, e.g., picture card or icon menu.
2. Perform a series of tasks in response to written instructions.	• Perform written direction sample worksheets across varying levels, found at: http://www.teach-nology.com/gold/new/directmiddle.html http://www.teach-nology.com/gold/new/directmiddle.html • Written direction sample worksheets across varying levels. • Give a student a LEGO box with directions or a simple item to construct (lamp, sheets on a bed, folder of papers, place setting, walking directions, etc.). • Have students reflect on what was easy/difficult with that task. - http://www.funenglishgames.com/writinggames/instructions.html • Written instruction games online for kids-functional!	• Student/teacher/family experiment with various types of written directions, for example, those with pictures (like building something) and those without (as in a manual).

Domain: Employment Skills
Competency: 20. Exhibiting Appropriate Employment Skills
Subcompetency: 89. Recognize the Importance of Attendance and Punctuality

Objectives	Activities/Strategies	Adult/Peer Roles
1. Identify reasons for good attendance and punctuality.	• Module with student questions at the end on punctuality on the worksite • Review tips for not being late: http://suite101.com/article/getting-to-work-on-time-a21768 • Review this lesson on work ethics: http://lor.gvtc.org/uploads/SEA165/player.html	• Teachers, peers, family support student's participation in these online activities and lessons. • Parents discuss attitudes toward people who are late.
2. Identify acceptable and unacceptable reasons for tardiness and absenteeism.	• Watch video on youtube of a girl who is late to work due to texting: http://www.youtube.com/watch?v=DV7Sv_WI3mM. • Ask employers acceptable and unacceptable reasons for tardiness. • Look in employee handbook to see the policies on tardiness. • Review video on punctuality as a sign of respect: http://www.youtube.com/watch?v=nyB_1Ng-QOI.	• Student, family, and community engage student with these important activities that are critical to successful employment. • Parents or peers discuss how tardiness and absenteeism may have caused problems for them.
3. Identify appropriate action to take if late or absent from work.	• Look in employee handbook or posting on the company's website about absenteeism. • Determine whether the employer provides paid time off or has guidelines and categories for missed days.	• Student and family explore job-related materials. • Students role-play what to do in the case of tardiness or absenteeism (e.g., call in, talk with supervisor, contact online, etc.).

EMPLOYMENT SKILLS

Domain: Employment Skills
Competency: 20. Exhibiting Appropriate Employment Skills
Subcompetency: 90. Recognize Importance of Supervision

Objectives	Activities/Strategies	Adult/Peer Roles
1. List roles and responsibilities of supervision.	• Review this article on the importance of workplace supervision: http://www.safetyxchange.org/training-and-leadership/effective-supervision-reduces-workplace-stress (article about the importance of supervision) • List the roles of people who currently supervise students (parents, teachers, older siblings, family members, bus driver, police, etc.). What would happen if they weren't there? • Look at a handbook to see the job description of a supervisor's role.	• Student, community, and family role-play situations involving a supervisor and supervisee, alternating roles.
2. Identify the appropriate response to a supervisory instruction.	• Role-playing	• Teacher, student, peers view video training and engage in role-play situations.
3. Complete a job following a supervisor's instructions.		• Support student in workplace and community settings. • During a job shadow, have a supervisor give directions for a task and the student follows them.

Domain: Employment Skills
Competency: 20. Exhibiting Appropriate Employment Skills
Subcompetency: 91. Demonstrate Knowledge of Workplace Safety

Objectives	Activities/Strategies	Adult/Peer Roles
1. Identify potential safety hazards on the job.	• Look at pictures of job sites and safety signs to identify potential hazards. • Show pictures of safety signs and define what they mean at http://www.compliancesigns.com/. • Walk through a job site and identify safety signs and safety precautions (hard hats, cones, safety glasses, gloves, etc.) as well as potential safety concerns.	• Student and peers discuss safety standards required on jobs.
2. Identify jobs that require safety equipment and identify the equipment.	• Identify a desired job and search internet resources about the safety equipment necessary for that job. • Discuss the safety equipment on webpage: http://www.professionalequipment.com/safety-products. • Walk through a job site and identify the equipment being used. • Sit through a training at a job site (OSHA training).	• Student and peers create slide show or bulletin board of varying jobs and safety equipment necessary to do the job.
3. Identify the main reasons for practicing safety on the job.	• Watch this YouTube video showing employees misusing office materials and creating a dangerous environment: http://www.youtube.com/watch?v=avB8Y-9BgYE. • Watch this whimsical YouTube video on using equipment safely: http://www.youtube.com/watch?v=I8uuFbJjAIQ&feature=related. • Watch and discuss this YouTube video on accidents in the workplace: http://www.youtube.com/watch?v=gYwMhepuJMA&feature=related.	• Student and peers role-play situations in which safety precautions are not observed and potential dangers that may result.
4. Follow safety instructions on the job (e.g., wear rubber gloves, safety goggles).	• Tour a job site and follow the instructions on safety from the supervisor. • Practice putting on gloves and taking off gloves in a safe way (assuming contamination).	• Occupational safety specialist describes how to identify and deal with potential safety hazards.

EMPLOYMENT SKILLS

Domain: Employment Skills
Competency: 20. Exhibiting Appropriate Employment Skills
Subcompetency: 92. Work With Others

Objectives	Activities/Strategies	Adult/Peer Roles
1. Identify reasons for working with others.	• Students make a list of reasons why and why not they would like to work with others. • For inspiration, watch this video on the teamwork of geese: watch a video on the teamwork of geese for inspiration: http://www.youtube.com/watch?v=8tz1IgB6IeA.	• Students engage in team games. • Students and peers identify situation in which there is cooperation and shared responsibility. • A coach discusses the importance of cooperation in athletics.
2. Identify the importance of individual components of a cooperative effort.	• Make a list of how the student can be a team player at the workplace. • Assign students to work together on a single task; provide roles and responsibilities that promote interdependence. • Students demonstrate the dependence of the group on individuals by participating in a simulated activity in which one member leaves or doesn't cooperate.	• Parents discuss ways their own jobs require teamwork.
3. Complete a task working with other persons.		• Play a game with a group of friends. • Cook dinner with a family member. • Plan a party with a friend or family member. • Student athletes discuss how they learned cooperation on the playing field. • Workers from the community discuss aspects of cooperation in their jobs. • Parents or peers work with the student to complete various household tasks. • Parents or peers discuss with the student what role each will assume in completing a task. • Peers engage in games or sports with the student.

EMPLOYMENT SKILLS

Domain: Employment Skills
Competency: 20. Exhibiting Appropriate Employment Skills
Subcompetency: 93. Meets Demands of Quality Work

Objectives	Activities/Strategies	Adult/Peer Roles
1. Identify minimum quality standards for various jobs.	• Industry representative leads discussions about their quality standards. • Class utilizes community-based instruction to observe quality control in various work environments.	• Parents discuss with students the dangers of producing inferior products.
2. Identify reasons for quality standards.	• Students discuss possible results of failure to maintain quality standards in specific jobs, for example, shoddy clothing or spoiled food. • Students describe minimum quality standards for earning academic grades. • Students identify and list minimum quality standards associated with a particular task, activity, or job in multiple environments, e.g., school lunch room, school wood shop, grocery store, public library, etc.	• Quality control professional explains his or her job and why it's important. • Parents and peers discuss standards which must be met on their jobs.
3. Perform simulated work tasks that have quality standards.	• Students observe a task or job being performed according to minimum quality standards. • Students participate in regular vocational training or work study to get practice in meeting and maintaining minimum quality standards.	• Workers discuss major reasons for minimum quality standards on the job. • Quality control expert explains his or her job and why it is important. • Parents or peers discuss standards which must be met on their jobs. • Consumer expert discusses quality control and its importance to the consumer. • Employment service counselor discusses the relationship of ability to meet minimum quality standards and employment. • Parents or peers give the student feedback on performance, with suggestions for improvement.

EMPLOYMENT SKILLS

Domain: Employment Skills
Competency: 20. Exhibiting Appropriate Employment Skills
Subcompetency: 94. Work at Expected Levels of Productivity

Objectives	Activities/Strategies	Adult/Peer Roles
1. Identify the need for performing jobs at expected levels of productivity.	• Go to the following website and review ways to boost your productivity: http://blog.intuit.com/employees/4-ways-to-boost-your-productivity-levels/. • Class takes a field trip or community-based instruction to local industries and businesses to observe quality control.	• Teachers, peers, and families discuss the dangers of producing inferior products with the student.
2. Identify expected levels of productivity required for specific jobs.	• Pick a specific job and list the expected levels of productivity. • Contact an employer about expected levels.	• Teachers and peers create a class compendium of expected levels of productivity required for specific jobs to keep as an employment resource to be updated as needed.
3. List reasons why a job must be performed at a certain rate of speed.	• Make a list of reasons why a job is performed at a certain speed • Make a plan of how students will meet that goal.	• Students observe a task or job being performed according to minimum quality standards. These jobs can be either in the school (professional, food service, administrative, custodial, etc) or within the local community • Students evaluate their ability and skills to do a similar task, listed above.
4. Perform a job at expected levels of productivity.	• Practice completing a task from above at a desired speed.	• Students perform jobs in the classroom in which the class has set standards and evaluates each other's performance. • Students participate in regular vocational training or work study to get practice in meeting, maintaining, or exceeding minimum quality standards.

Chapter 4
ASSESSMENTS AND IEP DEVELOPMENT

E valuation of student competency and establishing meaningful baseline data for intervention is a benchmark of providing targeted, appropriate instruction. Today, one can choose from thousands of available tests purporting to measure almost everything. With the advent of transition education, educators have turned their attention more to goals and interventions that cannot be measured by traditional evaluation instruments. Increased competence in caring for one's daily needs will probably not be reflected in an IQ score or in the results of achievement batteries. Neither will a greater understanding of the world of work or awareness of one's occupational interests. Therefore, an educator dealing with the transition education of a student is faced first with establishing goals and then with determining the extent to which these goals have been attained. Indeed, the law is clear that transition planning must be represented by "… appropriate measurable postsecondary goals *based upon age appropriate transition assessments* related to training, education, employment, and, where appropriate, independent living skills … and the transition services (including courses of study) needed to assist the child in reaching these goals." (Section 1414[d] [1] [A]).

The 20 life centered competencies relate directly to the concept of transition education. The behavioral objectives for the competency units represent tasks the student should be able to perform in order to demonstrate competence. This approach provides the educator with a relatively comprehensive set of goals for career education. The task remains to determine an appropriate evaluation system to measure student attainment and progress. Although many objectives can be evaluated by commercially available tests, it is doubtful that any test or battery of tests will adequately evaluate all objectives.

Because traditional psychometric techniques have limited usefulness in evaluating student achievement, particularly in areas related to transition education, alternative approaches are required. An alternative is to directly observe student performance on relevant tasks in a systematic, standardized manner. In a competency-based curriculum, learning can be measured best by comparing students to themselves as opposed to comparing them to other students. This is especially important in evaluating students with disabilities, since their progress may not reflect gains typically sought with other youngsters. Small improvements may represent major accomplishments. A method of evaluation is needed in which students can demonstrate progress in many areas. A philosophical position recognizing the importance of independent living skills and the value of small increments in improvement is also required. To that end, the Life Centered Education (LCE) curriculum provides assessment tools that are not only useful in building profiles of students' knowledge and performance, but also are directly linked to instructional components of the curriculum.

THE COMPETENCY RATING SCALE (CRS)

The Competency Rating Scale (CRS), presented in Appendix A, has been developed as a systematic approach to organizing and standardizing the assessment of students in the LCE curriculum.

The CRS is a rating scale built around the 20 competencies and 94 subcompetencies. These subcompetencies serve as the actual CRS items. The instructions present several behavioral criteria to use in judging student mastery of a subcompetency. Students are rated by the person most knowledgeable about their performance in a specific area, usually a teacher.

The use of specific behavioral criteria and precise definition of rating values is intended to enhance the reliability and validity of the ratings. Original criteria were reviewed and rank-ordered by national education experts to determine the appropriateness of the criteria to a given subcompetency. The criteria (behavioral objectives) presented for each subcompetency in the CRS represent a revision of the original criteria using the rankings and suggestions of the expert reviewers. The instructions include descriptions of the types of information regarding performance needed to rate students, who should do the rating, when rating should be done, criteria for rating, a rating key defining numerical rating values, and CRS record forms for recording and summarizing ratings as well as recording demographic data. The CRS record forms are divided into the three career education domains (Daily Living Skills, Self-Determination and Interpersonal Skills, and Employment Skills) for convenience.

CRS users are encouraged to perform an initial rating to be followed by at least annual one re-administration per year. The rater can assign ratings of the degree of mastery (0 = Not Competent, 1 = Partially Competent, 2 = Competent) for each subcompetency using the suggested behavioral criteria. Ratings are recorded and summarized on the appropriate CRS record forms. Results of CRS ratings can be used to develop individualized curricula. Following implementation of individualized curricula, the CRS can be used to evaluate program effectiveness.

Both the Knowledge Battery and Peformance Battery were updated and part of the development of the LCE web portal. Each of these is described in this chapter. *Please note that the primary use of the CRS is as a screening tool to give a more holistic, observation-based nuance to the assessment of student skill competence, and is not linked directly to instructional materials. It is therefore not reported on the Student Competency Rating Scale, and is used at the discretion of the school professional.*

Knowledge Battery

The Knowledge Battery is a standardized criterion-referenced instrument. It uses objective questions to assess students' knowledge in critical areas.

The Knowledge Battery consists of over 400 multiple-choice questions, which are broken down into three LCE domains: Daily Living Skills, Self-Determination and Interpersonal Skills, and Employment Skills. There are questions that address each of the LCE objectives. Each domain's section requires 1 to 3 hours to administer, depending on the ability level of the examinees.

Instructional objectives of the LCE curriculum were used as guidelines for the development of Knowledge Battery test items. The instructional objectives define the important content areas of the curriculum and provide a basis for the development of test items to ensure comprehensive treatment of each subcompetency area. Matching curriculum objectives to questions allows a more granular level of assessment of student knowledge.

The computer-based Knowledge Battery is designed for single or small-group administration. The optimal group size is six to eight students. If larger groups are tested — even using proctors — the performance of examinees, especially students with mild intellectual disabilities, will be a lower and less accurate assessment of their true skills. Instructions for administration, including audio-recorded delivery of questions for nonreaders, are given in the Knowledge Battery links. Results are automatically transferred to the Student Competency Assessment Report, allowing the school professional to view a knowledge profile for each student.

LCE Performance Battery

The Performance Battery also addresses all 20 competency areas. It is predicated on the concept that knowledge of a concept is inadequate unless it results in the ability to carry out the intrinsic skills. Since it would be extremely time-consuming to require students to actually perform/demonstrate every competency area in the multitude of situations and settings that will be needed, a worksheet approach to ascertaining competency mastery was used in many areas. However, they are equally balanced with demonstration, role-play, and other techniques that allow the student to depict the ability to carry out the skill, either partially or completely.

As with the Knowledge Battery, the instructional objectives of the curriculum guide were used as guidelines to develop the Performance Battery test items.

The Performance Battery should be administered to small groups of six to eight students so the examiner can attend to the student's questions regarding items. Items should be presented verbally to the students as they read along on the worksheets. Similar procedures to those outlined in the Knowledge Battery for preparation for test administration should be followed.

Each competency test specifies the materials needed for giving the tests, some general instructions to the examiner, and the instructions to give to the students. It is permissible to explain certain words that students do not understand, as long as the examiner does not give away the answers. The number of materials the examiner will have to secure to administer the various tests has been minimized. However, in some instances, there are several items that must be available.

The LCE Competency Batteries are unique in that they offer comprehensive, curriculum-based assessment (CBA) measures of student competence in the areas of Daily Living Skills, Self-Determination and Interpersonal Skills, and Employment Skills. There are few comprehensive measures of this nature relating directly to a specific curriculum. Thus, we believe educators will find this to be a very useful tool in their efforts to provide more extensive career development for their students.

USE OF THE LCE IN DEVELOPING INDIVIDUAL EDUCATION PLANS

The curriculum materials do not model a set template for IEP goal and objective development, due to the variability of forms and formats used across states and districts. Further, although IDEA 1997 mandated that IEPs include a "statement of measurable annual goals, including benchmarks or short-term objectives," IDEA 2004 eliminated the requirements for "benchmarks and short-term objectives" in IEPs, with the exception of IEPs of children who take alternate assessments, which must include "a description of benchmarks or short-term objectives" (Section 1414[d][1][A]).

As stated earlier, teams addressing transition planning must develop appropriate measurable postsecondary goals. Because of the thoroughness of LCE's assessment tools, data are available to provide performance snapshots to guide the development of IEP goals and objectives (as appropriate).

The function of the Knowledge Battery and Performance Battery assessments (and, peripherally, the CRS) is to provide direct data that will support the development of those measurable goals. The results give information about the competency, the subcompetency, and the objective levels. Because there is such granularity of data, there are several ways to use it as baseline data upon which to build effective instructional goals and/or objectives. Because the assessment data represents student knowledge at the subcompetency and objective levels, lower performance in particular competencies overall would target appropriate yearly IEP goals for that student and provide baseline data to sustain the goal's measurability and monitor student progress after instruction. For students, whose IEPs, per federal, state, and local definition, require short–term objectives to accompany the yearly goal, the data also exists from the Knowledge Battery at the level of the objectives that are housed under each subcompetency. Therefore, the assessment data from the objective level would support measurable short-term objectives in the IEP as well as a venue for retesting and progress monitoring formatively as the short-term objectives are being addressed instructionally. While Performance Battery data are available only at the competency level, the assumption is that a student completing an assessment of that competency on the Performance Battery has already performed at mastery on the Knowledge Battery. Therefore, any goal that is built from the Performance Battery data should reflect a practical, authentic use of a skill.

For students with more significant disabilities, it may be necessary to migrate further in creating goals and objectives. In this case, it may be advisable to use the Knowledge Battery data from the curriculum objective level to create the yearly goal, and, based on accompanying LCE instructional materials, use a task-analytic approach in setting the short-term objectives.

While this outlines the use of the Knowledge Battery and Performance Battery in creating measurable goals and objectives in the IEP, one should not discount the value of the information obtained from the optional CRS. While it does yield observational data sets rather than student performance data sets, it should still be considered a valuable component that can provide or even enhance baseline data provided through the student-completed Knowledge Battery and Performance Battery.

Appendix
COMPETENCY RATING SCALE MANUAL

COMPETENCY RATING SCALE MANUAL

The life-centered approach to career education bases its curriculum on 20 competencies that have been identified as necessary for personal independence in the community and on the job (Brolin, 1974). These 20 competencies have been further delineated into subcompetencies in its revised edition. If this curriculum is to be used, a uniform method of evaluating student performance and progress in career education is needed. Although there are numerous educational and psychological devices and systems in existence for evaluating student performance in a variety of areas, none appears to be sufficiently specific or comprehensive for the criteria that define the subcompetencies. The Competency Rating Scale (CRS) is an initial attempt to meet this need by providing educators with a systematic means of assessing student mastery of the subcompetencies. The purpose of this manual is to furnish the user with a guide for rating student performance for each subcompetency, as well as a comprehensive explanation of each subcompetency.

The CRS is a rating scale that the user completes by judging a student's mastery of the sub competencies using the criteria presented in Chapter 3 of this manual. Like any assessment device or system, the CRS requires a certain degree of training of the rater before actual use with students. Since the CRS requires judgments regarding student performance and behavior, it is necessary that all raters employ the same criteria when making judgments. This is critical if the user intends to compare students to one another or to evaluate changes in individual performance or behavior over time.

The manual is divided into four sections. Section I describes the rating key and how to rate student performance and behavior. Section II explains the use of the CRS Record Form. Section III presents explanations and behavioral criteria for the subcompetencies. Section IV describes interpretation of CRS results.

The task of assessing student performance in any subject area is a difficult one. This task becomes increasingly difficult for the educator dealing with the career education of students with disabilities.

SECTION I — RATING STUDENT PERFORMANCE

The Rating Key

The CRS provides four alternative ratings for student performance on each subcompetency. There are three sources from which the user can draw information to establish the rating for a given subcompetency. The most valid source of information is the rater's immediate personal observation of student performance and behavior. The rater's personal records or notes regarding student performance and behavior are probably less valid, but acceptable. Finally, written or verbal reports from other personnel are the least valid source of information, but they may be necessary.

When sufficient information exists to rate a subcompetency, one of the following ratings should be selected:

0 =   *Not Competent.* The student is unable to perform any of the behavioral criteria for the subcompetency. This rating should be used for students who, in the judgment of the rater, cannot be expected to perform this subcompetency satisfactorily for independent living. Such a student will require special help to master the subcompetency or, if not scheduled for further formal education, will require assistance from public or private individuals or agencies to accomplish the behavioral criteria.

1 =   *Partially Competent.* The student is able to perform at least one but not all of the behavioral criteria for the subcompetency. This rating should be used for students who, in the judgment of the rater, can be expected to perform this subcompetency satisfactorily for independent living following normal teaching intervention during formal education. Such a student might require assistance from public or private individuals or agencies if he or she is not scheduled for further formal education.

2 =   *Competent.* The student is able to perform all the behavioral criteria for the subcompetency. This rating should be used only for those students who, in the judgment of the rater, are able to perform the behavioral criteria satisfactorily for independent living without assistance or further formal education.

NR = *Not Rated.* The rater should use this rating for subcompetencies he or she is unable to rate due to absence of sufficient information or other logistical difficulty such as insufficient time.

If, at the time a student is scheduled to discontinue formal education, that student is not capable of independently performing the behavioral criteria for a subcompetency, the rater should determine whether or not the student could accomplish the subcompetency with assistance from others normally available in the student's environment. This is a yes or no decision and is further explained in Section II.

The Rater

Optimally, the same individual should rate a student's performance and behavior for all of the subcompetencies. However, logistical difficulties may preclude this. For this reason, the subcompetencies are separated into the three Life Centered Career Education domains: Daily Living Skills, Self-Determination and Interpersonal Skills, and Employment Skills (Section III). The CRS Record Form (Section II) is also separated into these three domains. It is highly desirable that the same individual rate all subcompetencies in a particular domain. If this type of procedure is not possible, one individual should be designated to coordinate the ratings of more than one rater within a domain. If more than one rater is employed, the coordinator should take care to ensure that these raters strictly adhere to the behavioral criteria for the subcompetencies. It is particularly important that ratings be as precise and consistent as possible since CRS results may be used to develop and evaluate individualized education programs.

Rating Intervals

Space is provided on the CRS Record Form (Section II) for seven ratings. It is suggested that the CRS be administered at the beginning of grade 7 and at the end of grades 7, 8, 9, 10, 11, and 12 to establish initial functioning and to monitor changes in performance and behavior. (The CRS could be used at the elementary grade level too, if desired.) If the rater is unfamiliar with a student entering grade 7, rating should be postponed until adequate observation has taken place to ensure accurate ratings. If the CRS is employed after a student has completed any of the intermediate or secondary years, it is recommended that an initial rating be administered followed by yearly ratings. The user is free to administer the CRS as frequently as is deemed advisable. However, caution should be taken not to "teach for the test." In other words, ratings should not take place immediately after the student has been taught a subcompetency, unless the user intends to do further ratings. A single rating following instruction will provide little information regarding long-term mastery of the subcompetency.

SECTION II — USING THE CRS RECORD FORM

The CRS Record Form is separated into three sections corresponding to the three domains: Daily Living Skills, Self-Determination and Interpersonal Skills, and Employment Skills. Each part can be administered independently. As noted in Section I of the manual, it is desirable that one individual rate all subcompetencies in a particular domain. This is a matter that each user must determine depending on his or her particular situation. An initial rating at the beginning of grade 7 and annual ratings at the end of grades 7, 8, 9, 10, 11, and 12 are illustrated.

Identifying Information

The CRS Record Form provides space to record the student's name, date of birth, and sex. Space is also provided for the name and address of the student's school.

Directions

The directions for the CRS Record Form indicate that the user should choose one of the four possible ratings for each subcompetency. The numerical ratings should be recorded in the space to the right of the subcompetency. The NR rating should be assigned to items that are not rated. The subcompetencies are listed on the left side of the CRS Record Form and are grouped under the competencies. Space is provided at the head of each rating column to record the rater's name(s), the student's grade level, and the date(s) of the rating period. If the ratings are completed in a single day, only that date need be recorded. However, if the ratings require more than one day, the user should record both the beginning and ending dates. It is recommended that ratings be completed as quickly as possible (e.g., one day to one week).

A *yes/no* rating is possible in the final column on the right side of the CRS Record Form. This space is provided for the rater to indicate whether or not a student who is finishing formal education can perform unmastered subcompeteneies with the assistance of individuals normally present in his or her environment. This column needs to be completed only for subcompetencies assigned a final rating of 0 or 1. Place a check (✓) in the *yes* or *no* space if needed.

Space is provided following the listing of the subcompetencies for the total possible score if a student were assigned the highest rating for each subcompetency in a domain. The total possible score can be calculated by counting the number of rated items (N) and multiplying by the highest possible rating (2). Thus, total possible score (TPS) = N x 2. To the right of the total possible score, space is provided to record the student's total actual score (TAS), which is the sum of the ratings for all rated items. Space is provided below the TAS to record the average score per item (AS). The AS is calculated by dividing the TAS by N (thus, AS = TAS/N). Space is provided at the end of the Employment Skills section for a cumulative total possible score, a cumulative total actual score, and a cumulative average score. The cumulative TPS can be calculated by adding the TPSs for the three domains. *Please note that the TPS and the cumulative TPS must be calculated for each administration since the number of rated items may vary with each administration. The cumulative TAS can be calculated by adding the TASs from the three domains. The cumulative AS can be calculated by adding the ASs from the three domains and dividing by 3. Thus, the user can evaluate performance and behavior for each domain as well as the three domains combined. There is space provided for comments at the end of each Record.*

SECTION III — BEHAVIORAL CRITERIA FOR RATING SUBCOMPETENCIES

A list of the 94 subcompetencies grouped into the three career education domains follows. Each subcompetency is described conceptually and further defined by behavioral criteria. A rank ordering of the criteria for each subcompetency in order of importance for the subcompetency was performed by five national education experts. Further revision of the original criteria considered clarity and specificity. As discussed in Section I, the rater should compare student performance to the behavioral criteria for each subcompetency to determine the degree of mastery. The ratings from the rating key can then be assigned to each subcompetency (item) based on the number of criteria that the student is able to perform for each subcompetency.

DAILY LIVING SKILLS

1. Managing Personal Finances

1. Identify money and make correct change
1. Identify coins and bills less than or equal to $100.00 in value.
2. Count money in coin and bill denominations with sums less than or equal to $20.00.
3. Make correct change from both bills and coins for amounts less than or equal to $50.00.

2. Make responsible expenditures
1. Identify prices on labels and tags on merchandise.
2. Choose most economical buy among like items of a similar quality.
3. Identify purchases as necessities or luxuries in the areas of food, clothing, housing, and transportation.
4. Determine amount of money saved by buying sale items.
5. Compare prices of an item in three stores.

3. Keep basic financial records
1. Construct a monthly personal budget for your present income.
2. Identify financial information and financial records that should be retained.
3. Record personal major income and expenses for 1 month.
4. Calculate balances of major income and expenses for 1 month .
5. List basic terms used in keeping financial records.

4. Calculate and pay taxes
1. Know types of taxes normally assessed in the geographic area.
2. Know penalties and deadlines for the payment of taxes.
3. Know sources of assistance for the filing of taxes.
4. Complete a 1040 tax form.

5. Use credit responsibly
1. Identify resources for obtaining a loan.
2. Name advantages and disadvantages of using credit cards.
3. Complete a loan application.

6. Use banking services
1. Open a checking account.
2. Open a savings account.
3. Write checks, make deposits, and record checking transactions.
4. Make deposits and withdrawals, and record savings transactions.
5. Use local and online banking.

2. Selecting and Managing a Household

7. Select adequate housing
1. List personal or family housing requirements, including space, location, and yard.
2. Identify different types of housing available in the community.

     3. Identify advantages and disadvantages of different types of housing.

     4. Identify procedures for renting a house or apartment.

     5. Identify procedures for buying a house.

8. Set up a household

     1. Describe procedures for connecting utility services.

     2. Acquire basic household items.

     3. Acquire furniture and major appliances.

9. Maintain home exterior/interior

     1. Identify basic appliances and tools used in exterior maintenance.

     2. List routine cleaning and maintenance activities.

     3. Outline a weekly housekeeping routine.

     4. Identify the uses of common household cleaning products and equipment.

     5. Accessing assistance services and putting in work orders.

     6. Dispose of household refuse properly.

     7. Secure home when at home and away from home.

10. Use basic appliances and tools

     1. Name common appliances and tools found in the home and tell how each is used.

     2. Demonstrate appropriate use of basic appliances and tools.

     3. Name safety procedures to follow when using appliances and tools.

     4. Perform basic home care tasks.

3. Caring for Personal Needs

11. Obtain, interpret, and understand health information

     1. Understand preventive physical and mental health measures, including proper diet, nutrition, exercise, and stress reduction.

     2. Using available information to make appropriate health-related decisions.

     3. Establishing and monitoring personal and family health goals.

12. Demonstrate knowledge of physical fitness, nutrition, and weight

     1. Know ways nutrition relates to health.

     2. Know a meal balanced for nutritional and caloric content.

     3. Know ways in which exercise relates to health.

     4. Identify and demonstrate correct ways of performing common physical exercises.

     5. Develop and practice a personal physical fitness routine.

13. Exhibit proper grooming and hygiene

     1. Demonstrate basic aspects of proper hygiene.

     2. Identify proper grooming.

     3. Identify proper products for hygiene and where to obtain them.

     4. Identify proper products for grooming and where to obtain them.

14. Dress appropriately
1. List clothing appropriate for different weather conditions.
2. List clothing appropriate for different activities.
3. Given an occasion, choose the appropriate clothing to be worn.

15. Demonstrate knowledge of common illness, prevention, and treatment
1. Identify major symptoms of common illnesses.
2. Teach how cleanliness is related to health.
3. Locate sources of assistance with medical problems.
4. Identify dosage information from a medicine bottle label.
5. List common medicines found in the home and their uses.

16. Practice personal safety
1. Identify ways to secure home from intruders.
2. Identify things to do to avoid personal assault.
3. Identify and demonstrate self-protection or self-defense behaviors and techniques.
4. Identify precautions to follow when dealing with strangers.
5. Identify potential safety hazards in the home.
6. List and demonstrate actions to take in the event of an emergency.

4. Demonstrating Relationship Responsibilities

17. Understand relationship roles and changes with friends and others
1. Identify reasons for establishing relationships.
2. Identify personal responsibilities in relationships.
3. Identify joint responsibility in relationships.
4. Demonstrate effective relationships with friends and others.

18. Understand relationship roles and changes within the family
1. Identify reasons for establishing relationships.
2. Identify personal responsibilities in relationships.
3. Identify joint responsibility in relationships.
4. Demonstrate effective relationships with families.
5. Identify changes when a child enters the family.
6. Identify common family challenges and a positive way of meeting those challenges.

19. Demonstrate care of children
1. List the physical and psychological responsibilities involved in child care.
2. Identify basic stages of child development and a characteristic of each.
3. Identify potential dangers and required safety measures.
4. Demonstrate procedures for care of a child's physical health and identify common childhood illnesses, symptoms, and treatment.
5. Identify parental responsibilities involved in the psychological care of the child.

5. Buying, Preparing, and Consuming Food

20. Plan/eat balanced meals
    1. List the basic food groups required in each meal.
    2. Identify appropriate foods eaten at typical daily meals.
    3. Plan a day's balanced meals within a given budget.
21. Purchase food
    1. Create a weekly shopping list and purchase within a budget.
    2. List characteristics of perishable foods.
    3. Identify types and cuts of meat, fish, poultry, and vegetarian proteins.
    4. Identify how to use ads and coupons to take advantage of sales.
22. Store food
    1. Identify the need for proper food storage.
    2. Identify and demonstrate appropriate food storage techniques.
    3. Identify appearance of foods when they have spoiled.
23. Clean food preparation areas
    1. Identify the importance of personal hygiene in food preparation areas.
    2. List reasons for cleaning work area and materials after food preparation.
    3. Identify and demonstrate appropriate cleaning procedures.
    4. Identify and demonstrate appropriate waste disposal procedures.
24. Preparing meals and cleaning up after dining
    1. Identify food preparation procedures.
    2. Identify and demonstrate the use of basic appliances and tools.
    3. List basic recipe abbreviations and cooking terms.
    4. Practice kitchen safety procedures.
    5. Prepare a full-course meal for one or more people.
    6. Cleaning up and doing the dishes after dining.
25. Demonstrate appropriate eating habits
    1. Identify and demonstrate the proper way to set a table and serve food.
    2. Identify and demonstrate proper manners and eating behavior at a meal.
    3. Identify and demonstrate proper manners and eating behavior at home or in the community.

6. Buying and Caring for Clothing

26. Wash/clean clothing
    1. Identify the following laundry products and their uses: bleaches, detergents, and fabric softeners.
    2. Identify and demonstrate appropriate laundering procedures for different types of clothing.
    3. Demonstrate use of laundry facilities at a laundromat.
27. Purchase clothing
    1. List basic articles of clothing.
    2. Identify personal body measurements and clothing sizes.

3. List major clothing categories by dress, work, casual, sports, and school.
4. Given a hypothetical budget, select a school wardrobe.
5. State the importance of matching colors and fabrics.

28. Iron, mend, and store clothing
1. Identify and demonstrate proper ironing procedures for common fabrics.
2. Demonstrate appropriate safety precautions for using ironing equipment.
3. Identify when, how, and where to store clothing.
4. Identify and demonstrate procedures for mending clothing.

7. Exhibiting Responsible Citizenship

29. Demonstrate knowledge of civil rights and responsibilities
1. Identify basic civil rights when being questioned by law enforcement officials.
2. Locate resources where one can acquire legal aid.
3. Identify actions to take when a crime has been witnessed.
4. List basic civil rights.
5. Identify who must register with the Selective Service.
6. Identify when eligible individuals must register.
7. Locate the address of the Selective Service or recruitment office nearest the student's home.

30. Know nature of local, state, and federal governments
1. Identify the purpose of government.
2. Define democracy and representative government.
3. Identify the branches of government, their functions, and one major official of each branch of government.
4. Identify one way states might be different without a federal government.
5. Identify one duty of each level of government.

31. Demonstrate knowledge of the law and ability to follow the law
1. List types of local laws.
2. Identify possible consequences of violating laws.
3. List basic reasons for government and laws.
4. Explain and demonstrate the basic court system and its procedures.

32. Demonstrate knowledge of citizen rights and responsibilities
1. Locate community services available to citizens.
2. List major responsibilities of citizens.
3. Identify voting requirements and demonstrate procedures.
4. Identify why it is important to be an informed voter.
5. List the dates for primary and general elections, and demonstrate procedures for registration.
6. Identify sources that inform the voter about election issues.

8. Utilizing Recreational Facilities and Engaging in Leisure

33. Demonstrate knowledge of available community resources
    1. List sources of information about specific recreational activities.
    2. List activities appropriate to each season of the year.
    3. Locate recreational and facilities and equipment in the community.
    4. Participate in recreational activities outside the home.
34. Choose and plan activities
    1. List personal leisure activities.
    2. List the costs, times, locations, and physical requirements of activities.
    3. Develop individual plan of leisure activities.
35. Demonstrate knowledge of the value of recreation
    1. List differences between leisure that involves nonpaid work activity and relaxation.
    2. List ways in which recreation affects both physical and mental health.
    3. List personal requirements of leisure time.
36. Engage in group and individual activities
    1. Identify reasons for participating in group activities.
    2. Identify and demonstrate knowledge of rules of group activities.
    3. List qualities of good sportsmanship.
    4. Identify and demonstrate the proper care of sports equipment.
    5. Identify general safety rules of physical activities.
    6. Plan recreational/leisure activities time.
37. Plan recreation and leisure activities
    1. Demonstrate knowledge of available community resources.
    2. Choose and plan activities.
    3. Demonstrate knowledge of the value of recreation.
    4. Engage in group and individual activities.
    5. Adopt and care for pets.
    6. Tips to pool, day trips, classes.

9. Choosing and Accessing Transportation

38. Demonstrate knowledge of traffic rules and safety
    1. Identify the purpose and demonstrate procedures for pedestrian safety signs.
    2. List reasons for common traffic and safety rules and practices.
    3. Identify vehicle safety signs included on the driver's education test.
39. Demonstrate knowledge and use of various means of transportation
    1. Identify types of transportation available in the community.
    2. Identify reasons transportation is needed and what kind is most appropriate.
    3. Identify and demonstrate procedures to take a train, interstate bus, taxi, and airplane.
40. Find way around the community
    1. Given a picture of a numbered house, identify numbers of houses on either side.

    2. Given city and state maps, identify directions, symbols, and distance.

    3. Identify basic community resources.

41. Drive a car

    1. Demonstrate knowledge of appropriate driving techniques for different kinds of driving conditions and problems that could arise because of weather.

    2. Describe appropriate procedures to follow after being involved in an accident.

    3. Identify everyday basic driving knowledge.

    4. Demonstrate proficiency on the written portion of the operator's exam.

SELF-DETERMINATION AND INTERPERSONAL SKILLS

10. Understanding Self-Determination

42. Understand personal responsibility

    1. Identify areas of personal responsibility.

    2. List factors important in becoming personally responsible in one's life.

    3. Identify reasons for being personally responsible.

    4. Identify ways that personal responsibility affects present and future outcomes in life.

43. Identify and understand motivation

    1. Identify and describe areas of self-motivation.

    2. List appropriate ways to motivate yourself and others.

    3. Identify how motivation affects present and future goal attainment.

44. Anticipate consequences to choices

    1. Describe consequences or outcomes of personal choices.

    2. List and demonstrate knowledge of ways in which personal choices produce consequences.

    3. Describe the concept of maximum gain for minimum risk in making personal choices.

45. Communicate needs

    1. Identify communication skills necessary in becoming self-determined.

    2. Demonstrate appropriate communication skills at home, at work, and in the community.

    3. Identify ways to communicate effectively at home, at work, and in the community.

    4. Demonstrate assertive communication when problem solving and resolving conflicts.

11. Being Self-Aware

46. Understand personal characteristics and needs

    1. Understand physical characteristics.

    2. Identify emotions.

    3. Understand the effect of emotions and choices.

    4. Identify interest and abilities.

    5. Identify character traits.

6. Identify current roles.

7. Identify possible future roles.

8. Understand emotional and physical self-awareness as a component of self-determination.

47. *Identify needs*

1. Identify physical needs.

2. Identify emotional needs.

3. Identify social needs (communication, acceptance, respect, etc.).

4. Identify educational needs (study skills, organizational skills, executive functioning).

48. *Identify preferences.*

1. Distinguish between needs and preferences.

2. Identify physical preferences.

3. Identify emotional preferences.

4. Identify social preferences.

5. Identify educational preferences.

49. *Describe others' perception of oneself.*

1. List potential reactions of others to oneself.

2. Construct a personal view of how others see oneself.

3. Describe the relationship between one's own behaviors and others' reactions.

4. Demonstrate awareness of individual differences in others.

50. *Demonstrate awareness of how one's behavior affects others*

1. List ways in which behavior affects others around us.

2. List appropriate behaviors for a variety of situations.

3. List different cues elicited by others that behavior is inappropriate.

4. List ways to correct inappropriate behavior.

12. Developing Interpersonal Skills

51. *Demonstrating listening and responding skills*

1. Demonstrate appropriate listening and responding behaviors.

2. Identify positive and negative outcomes associate with listening and responding.

52. *Establish and maintain close relationships*

1. Identify qualities of an individual who would be desirable as a dating partner.

2. Identify and demonstrate appropriate procedures for making a date.

3. List activities that are appropriate for a date.

4. Identify characteristics of close relationships.

5. List different types of close relationships.

6. Recognize and respond to the intimate feelings of others.

7. Identify persons with whom one could establish a close relationship.

53. *Make and maintain friendships*

1. Identify the necessary components of a friendship.

2. List personal considerations in choosing a friend.

3. List rights and responsibilities important in personal friendships.

4. List activities that can be shared with friends.

54. Develop and demonstrate appropriate behavior
    1. Identify and demonstrate good interpersonal skills.
    2. Identify ways in which one's behavior affects others.
    3. Identify cues presented by others that one's behavior is inappropriate.
    4. Identify ways to correct one's inappropriate behavior.

55. Accept and give praise and criticism
    1. Identify statements of praise in everyday activities.
    2. List appropriate and inappropriate responses to praise.
    3. Respond to praise statements by others.
    4. List the effects of praise on oneself.
    5. Identify critical and/or rejecting types of statements.
    6. List appropriate ways to respond to criticism and/or rejection.
    7. Respond appropriately to critical statements.
    8. List positive and negative effects of criticism.

13. Communicating With Others

56. Communicate with understanding
    1. Identify and demonstrate methods of speaking appropriately in social conversations.

57. Know subtleties of communication
    1. Identify and demonstrate subtle or nonverbal means of communication.
    2. Identify subtle verbal expressions that correspond to feelings.
    3. Identify verbal expressions that are inconsistent with feelings.
    4. Demonstrate subtle verbal and nonverbal elements of communication.

58. Assertive and effective communication
    1. Identify and demonstrate assertive communication behaviors.
    2. Identify assertive communication behaviors.
    3. Identify positive and negative outcomes associate with assertively communicating.

59. Recognize and respond to emergency situations
    1. Identify sights and sounds of emergency situations.
    2. Identify appropriate authorities to contact in emergency situations.
    3. Describe personal communication indicating emergency situations.
    4. List personal responsibilities in emergency situations.

14. Good Decision Making

60. Problem solving
    1. Identify a problem.
    2. Identify desired outcome.
    3. Identify resources necessary to attain desired outcome.
    4. Identify past experiences similar to this problem and describe outcome(s) .

61. Identify and set goals
   1. Identify ways goal setting and attainment can affect one's life.
   2. Identify potential goals.
   3. List possible outcomes to be considered when setting goals.
   4. Determining a plan of action.
62. Develop plans and attain goals
   1. Set one goal for school, home, and recreation.
   2. Set short-term and long-term personal goals.
   3. Identify characteristics of realistic goals.
   4. Identify appropriate individuals for obtaining assistance with setting and achieving goals.
   5. Identify potential barriers to goals.
   6. Set personal goals.
63. Self-evaluation and feedback
   1. Determine reasons why goal was or was not met.
   2. Determine positives and negatives of: problemsolving, goal setting and attainment, and independent performance.
64. Develop and evaluate alternatives
   1. Define the meaning of alternatives
   2. List possible alternatives with respect to a personal goal.
   3. Describe a compromise with respect to a personal goal.
   4. List resources for information that develops alternatives.

15. Developing Social Awareness

65. Develop respect for the rights and properties of others
   1. Identify personal and property rights of others.
   2. Identify a reason for respecting the rights and properties of others.
   3. Demonstrate respect for others and their property.
   4. List appropriate situations and procedures for borrowing the property of others.
66. Recognize authority and follow instructions
   1. Identify common authority roles.
   2. Identify aspects of following instructions.
   3. Identify situations in which the individual has the right to disregard instructions from authorities.
67. Demonstrate appropriate behavior in public settings
   1. Identify appropriate behavior in public places.
   2. Identify and demonstrate appropriate behaviors when using transportation facilities.
   3. Identify and demonstrate appropriate behaviors when using eating facilities.
   4. Identify and demonstrate appropriate behaviors when using recreational facilities.

68. Understand the motivations of others
    1. Identify and understand the motives of others in a given situation.
    2. Identify the ways in which others' motives affect their decision making.
    3. Incorporating the motives of others into one's decision making.

16. Understanding Disability Rights and Responsibilities

69. Identify and understand rights and responsibilities
    1. Identify specific details (i.e., legislation, social movements, etc.) regarding the United States' disability rights movement.
    2. Identify your disability rights based on your disability across settings (elementary, secondary, and postsecondary education, employment, nationally, etc.).
    3. Identify responsibilities to ensure your rights are not violated and what to do if they are violated.
    4. Demonstrate self-awareness through demonstrating disability rights and responsibilities knowledge.
70. Identify and appropriately access needed services and supports
    1. Identify needed services and supports to live successfully.
    2. Determine how to appropriately access disability needed services and supports.

EMPLOYMENT SKILLS

17. Knowing and Exploring Occupational Possibilities

71. Identify personal values met through work
    1. List economic reasons for working at a job.
    2. Identify how a job affects building personal and social relationships.
    3. Identify personal needs that can be met through work.
    4. Describe how work relates to one's self-esteem.
72. Identify societal values met through work
    1. Identify ways in which individual workers help society.
    2. Identify ways in which members of a specific occupation contribute to society.
    3. Identify ways in which workers on different jobs are interdependent.
    4. Describe ways society rewards different occupations.
73. Identify remunerative aspects of work
    1. Identify why people are paid for working.
    2. Identify why some jobs pay better than others.
    3. Discuss personal needs that are met through wages.
    4. Discuss positive and negative aspects of different kinds of wages.
    5. Given a paycheck stub, calculate deduction information.
74. Locate sources of employment and training information
    1. List sources of employment information.
    2. List information provided by the sources from objective 1.
    3. Locate sources of training information.

75. Classify jobs into employment categories
1. Locate jobs using Yellow Pages and want ads.
2. Locate occupational categories and sort jobs into different occupational categories.
3. Locate information about job classifications.
4. List major categories of jobs related to interest.
5. List general job categories.
6. Locate training requirements and wages for common job classifications.

76. Investigate local employment and training opportunities
1. Select an occupational area and find local employers in the Yellow Pages.
2. Collect and read help wanted ads in the occupational areas selected in objective 1.
3. Utilize sources of employment information.
4. Locate sources of employment information.

18. Exploring Employment Choices

77. Identify major employment interests
1. Identify occupational categories of interest.
2. Rank areas of personal interest in order of importance in finding an occupation.
3. Identify how interests relate to jobs.
4. Describe ways the chosen job of interest relates to future personal goals.

78. Identify employment aptitudes
1. Identify different aptitudes necessary in the performance of various jobs.
2. Identify personal aptitudes.
3. Identify activities that could improve personal aptitude necessary for a preferred job.

79. Investigate realistic employment choices
1. Identify jobs of interest.
2. Obtain specific information about jobs of interest.
3. Obtain observational information about jobs of interest through participation (e.g., on-site visits, work samples, job tryouts).
4. Identify a job that is commensurate with interests and abilities.

80. Identify requirements of desired and available employment
1. Identify the availability and location of jobs.
2. List specific job-related requirements.
3. Identify an alternative for each occupation for which personal qualifications are not commensurate with identified requirements.

81. Identify major employment needs
1. Identify needs that can be met through one's occupation and rank them in order of personal preference.
2. Identify personal-social needs met through work.
3. Name status needs met through work.
4. Identify factors that the student needs in a personal occupational environment.

5. Identify the most personally satisfying aspects and the least satisfying aspects about a specific job.
6. Identify criteria one would use in selecting an occupation.

19. Seeking, Securing, and Maintaining Employment

82. Search for a job
1. Identify the steps involved in searching for a job.
2. Identify a potential job through employment resources.
3. Arrange a real or simulated job interview.

83. Apply for a job
1. Identify appropriate job application procedures.
2. Collect a personal data sheet to be used for job application.
3. Complete a real or simulated job application with spelling assistance.
4. Apply for a real or simulated job in person or by telephone.

84. Interview for a job
1. Obtain an interview or carry out a mock interview.
2. Identify interview behaviors.
3. Complete a real or simulated job interview.
4. Obtain transportation to and from the interview.

85. Solve job-related problems
1. Identify potential problems encountered on the job.
2. For potential problems, identify possible solutions.
3. Identify resources for assistance if problems cannot be personally resolved.

86. Functions of meeting and exceeding job standards
1. Determine the competitive level of skill and performance required for essential functions of a specific job.
2. Identify potential remedial activities that might be required by an occupation.
3. Determine the level of personal abilities required for a specific occupation.

87. Maintain and advance in employment
1. Identify factors that determine successful maintenance of employment.
2. Identify factors that determine unsuccessful maintenance of employment.
3. Identify potential employment variations within a specific occupation.
4. Identify factors that lead to termination of employment.
5. Identify factors that lead to advancement in employment.

20. Exhibiting Appropriate Employment Skills

88. Follow directions and observe regulations
1. Perform a series of tasks in response to verbal instructions.
2. Perform a series of tasks in response to written instructions.

89. Recognize importance of attendance and punctuality
1. Identify reasons for good attendance and punctuality.
2. Identify acceptable and unacceptable reasons for tardiness and absenteeism.
3. Identify appropriate action to take if late or absent from work.

90. Recognize importance of supervision
  1. List roles and responsibilities of supervision.
  2. Identify the appropriate response to a supervisory instruction.
  3. Complete a job following a supervisor's instructions.
91. Demonstrate knowledge of workplace safety
  1. Identify potential safety hazards on the job.
  2. Identify jobs that require safety equipment and identify the equipment.
  3. Identify the main reasons for practicing safety on the job.
  4. Follow safety instructions on the job (e.g., wear rubber gloves, safety goggles).
92. Work with others
  1. Identify reasons for working with others.
  2. Identify the importance of individual components of a cooperative effort.
  3. Complete a task working with other persons.
93. Meet demands of quality work
  1. Identify minimum quality standards for various jobs.
  2. Identify reasons for quality standards.
  3. Perform simulated work tasks that have quality standards.
94. Work at expected levels of productivity
  1. Identify the need for performing jobs at expected levels of productivity.
  2. Identify expected levels of productivity required for specific jobs.
  3. List reasons why a job must be performed at a certain rate of speed.
  4. Perform a job at expected levels of productivity.

SECTION IV—INTERPRETATION

Although it would be ultimately desirable for each student to achieve 100% mastery, it is difficult to predict whether this goal can be attained in any present educational setting. Each user will be faced with determining whether complete mastery of a specified percentage of the subcompetencies is preferable to a partial mastery of all the subcompetencies. At this time, the suggested method in interpretation involves the user's identification of student strengths and weaknesses. Such identification should prove useful for developing individualized education programs (IEPs), as well as evaluating IEP outcomes. Since the CRS items are actually the subcompetencies of the Life Centered Curriculum, low-rated items can be used to establish short-term objectives for individualized planning. Re-administration of the CRS can then be used to evaluate the effectiveness of such planning by comparing pre- and post-intervention ratings.

The CRS user can review student performance and behavior for any given rating period to determine deficient areas. Such a determination can assist both in general curriculum planning and in individualized planning. If a large percentage of students are deficient in particular areas (subcompetencies, competencies, or domains), emphasis on these areas could be incorporated into general curriculum planning. Individual weaknesses can be remedied through revised IEPs. The user should be aware that the rating key allows only three numerical ratings. The operational definition of the 1 rating ("at least one, but not all") makes student progress on a subcompetency possible without a change in numerical rating. A student might require several years to progress from a rating of 1 on an individual subcompetency to a rating of 2. Therefore, in the IEP evaluation, the user should look for short-term gains in the larger categories (competencies or domains). The present system will reflect short-term gains when used in this manner.

The CRS user can review student performance and behavior over several rating periods to determine progress as well as establish realistic expectancies for typical student growth and development. This interpretation not only provides the user with suggestions for immediate curriculum planning on a general and individual basis, but also provides suggestions for long-range curriculum sequencing. This type of data should prove particularly useful after systematic analysis, since there is little information available to predict typical developmental stages in the career education of these students.

Although the identified subcompetencies, competencies, and domains are felt to be generally comprehensive, there is no evidence at present that these divisions and their sequencing correlate strongly with student ability to master these objectives at any particular age or developmental stage. Thus, the CRS user has an opportunity to either formally or informally establish expectancies and sequencing in each particular setting. In summary, the CRS user can employ results to:

- Determine individual student strengths and weaknesses.
- Develop and evaluate IEPs for individual students.
- Determine group strengths and weaknesses.
- Plan immediate curriculum for groups of students.
- Monitor individual and group progress.
- Establish empirically derived expectancies for individuals and groups.
- Establish empirically derived developmental stages for these students in career education.
- Develop curriculum sequencing and modification to relate to expectancies and developmental stages.